KT-569-890

SELECTED POEMS
STEVIE SMITH

Stevie Smith was born in Hull. When she was three she went with her mother and sister to live with her aunt in a house in Palmers Green, London, where she was to stay for the rest of her life. She attended the North London Collegiate School for Girls and her first and only job was with Newnes-Pearson, the magazine publishers, where she became private secretary to Sir George Newnes and Sir Neville Pearson. She submitted her first volume of poems to Jonathan Cape when she was thirty-two, but was asked to write a novel instead. Her first book, *Novel on Yellow Paper*, was published in 1936, and was followed the next year by a volume of poetry, *A Good Time was Had by All*; both books were immediately recognized as being the product of a unique talent. She wrote only two more novels, *Over the Frontier* (1938) and *The Holiday* (1949), but had a further eight collections of poems published, her reputation reaching its peak in the 1950s. She also made several very effective recordings and broadcasts of her poetry, reading and singing to her own music, largely based on Gregorian chant and hymn tunes.

Stevie Smith died in 1971 at the age of sixty-eight. In 1975 her *Collected Poems* were published and in 1977 Hugh Whitemore wrote *Stevie*, based on her life and writings and starring Glenda Jackson; the stageplay was later adapted into a successful film.

STEVIE SMITH·
SELECTED POEMS

*Edited with a Preface
by James MacGibbon*

PENGUIN BOOKS

Penguin Books Ltd, Harmondsworth, Middlesex. England
Penguin Books, 625 Madison Avenue, New York, New York 10022, U.S.A.
Penguin Books Australia Ltd, Ringwood, Victoria, Australia
Penguin Books Canada Ltd, 2801 John Street, Markham, Ontario, Canada L3R 1B4
Penguin Books (N.Z.) Ltd, 182–190 Wairau Road, Auckland 10, New Zealand

—

First published as *The Collected Poems of Stevie Smith* by Allen Lane 1975
This selection published in Penguin Books 1978

—

The Collected Poems of Stevie Smith Copyright © Stevie Smith, 1937,
1938, 1942, 1950, 1957, 1962, 1966, 1971, 1972
This arrangement Copyright © James MacGibbon, 1975, 1978
All rights reserved
Requests for permission to reprint should be sent to
James MacGibbon, The Cellars, Landscove, Ashburton, Devon TQ13 7LY

—

Made and printed in Great Britain by
Hazell Watson & Viney Ltd,
Aylesbury, Bucks
Set in Monotype Bembo

Except in the United States of America,
this book is sold subject to the condition
that it shall not, by way of trade or otherwise,
be lent, re-sold, hired out, or otherwise circulated
without the publisher's prior consent in any form of
binding or cover other than that in which it is
published and without a similar condition
including this condition being imposed
on the subsequent purchaser

To
Glenda Jackson and Hugh Whitemore
who achieved what seemed impossible –
the dramatic portrayal of
Stevie Smith

CONTENTS

PREFACE 17

The Hound of Ulster 21
On the Death of a German Philosopher 22
Papa Love Baby 22
Bandol (Var) 23
Egocentric 23
Alfred the Great 24
Mrs Simpkins 25
How far can you Press a Poet? 26
To the Tune of the Coventry Carol 26
The Suburban Classes 27
Spanish School 27
Night-Time in the Cemetery 29
Alone in the Woods 29
God and the Devil 30
Es war einmal 31
Numbers 32
From the County Lunatic Asylum 33
The Bereaved Swan 33
Correspondence between Mr Harrison in
    Newcastle and Mr Sholto Peach Harrison
    in Hull 34
Nature and Free Animals 35
Eng. 35
Death Bereaves our Common Mother
    Nature Grieves for my Dead Brother 36
Bag-Snatching in Dublin 36
The River Deben 37
Death Came to Me 38
No Respect 39

The Reason   40
I Like to Play with Him   40
Analysand   41
Sunt Leones   42
Lord Mope   43
Never Again   44
Little Boy Lost   44
Angel of Grace   45
Freddy   46
Is it Wise?   47
This Englishwoman   48
Lord Barrenstock   48
Maximilian Esterhazy   50
Major Macroo   50
Private Means is Dead   51
Bereavement   52
Death of Mr Mounsel   53
Who Killed Lawless Lean?   53
Road Up   54
Mrs Osmosis   55
The Fugitive's Ride   55
Suburb   57
Beware the Man   59
Breughel   60
Tender Only to One   61
O Happy Dogs of England   61
Darling Daughters   62
The Bishops of the Church of England   62
Eulenspiegelei   63
The Abominable Lake   64
One of Many   65
Death's Ostracism   65
The Boat   67
Parrot   67
The Doctor   68
I Hate this Girl   68
Infelice   69
Come, Death (I)   70

Silence and Tears	71
A Father for a Fool	72
Brickenden, Hertfordshire	72
The Murderer	74
Mother, among the Dustbins	74
Le Désert de l'Amour	75
To a Dead Vole	76
Reversionary	76
Dear Karl	76
In Canaan's Happy Land	78
Proud Death with Swelling Port	78
My Soul	79
Dear Female Heart	80
How Slowly Time Lengthens	80
The River Humber	81
La Gretchen de Nos Jours (I)	82
Nourish Me on an Egg	83
Souvenir de Monsieur Poop	83
Unser Vater	85
Gnädiges Fräulein	85
The Friend	86
The Lads of the Village	87
The Photograph	87
'. . . and the clouds return after the rain'	88
Out of Time	88
The Children of the Cross	90
Fallen, Fallen	90
Will Ever?	90
Little Boy Sick	91
The Violent Hand	92
Human Affection	92
A King in Funeral Procession	92
Murder	93
Girls!	94
Where are you going?	94
Autumn	95
Poet!	95
The Zoo	95

Advice to Young Children 97
The Face 97
If I lie down 98
Conviction (i) 98
Conviction (ii) 99
Conviction (iii) 99
Conviction (iv) 99
The Virtuoso 100
Villains 100
Le Majeur Ydow 100
The Little Daughters of America 101
She said ... 101
Quand on n'a pas ce que l'on aime, il faut
  aimer ce que l'on a – 101
The Conventionalist 101
Study to Deserve Death 102
Dirge 102
Distractions and the Human Crowd 103
Be off! 104
Love Me! 104
The Wild Dog 104
Lady 'Rogue' Singleton 105
Rencontres Funestes 105
The Film Star 106
The Bottle of Aspirins 106
The Governess 107
The Actress 108
The Devil-my-Wife 108
The Repentance of Lady T 108
The Smile 109
Forgot! 109
A Man I Am 110
The White Thought 111
In the Night 111
The Magic Morning 111
Après la Politique, la Haine des Bourbons 113
The Poets are Silent 113
The Pleasures of Friendship 113

Happiness	114
Lot's Wife	114
The Fool	115
No More People	115
Hast Du Dich Verirrt?	115
Satin-Clad	116
Unpopular, lonely and loving	116
'Ceci est digne de gens sans Dieu'	116
When the Sparrow Flies	116
Voices against England in the Night	117
'N'est-ce pas assez de ne me point haïr?'	118
The Failed Spirit	118
The Sliding Mountain	118
The Recluse	119
'I could let Tom go – but what about the children?'	119
Christmas	120
Torquemada	121
The Roman Road	121
The Castle	122
To Dean Inge Lecturing on Origen	123
Behind the Knight	123
Harold's Leap	124
A Mother's Hearse	124
Touch and Go	125
Man is a Spirit	127
Thought is Superior	128
The River God	128
Cool as a Cucumber	129
The Orphan Reformed	130
A Shooting Incident	130
'Oh stubborn race of Cadmus' seed . . .'	134
The Ambassador	134
Persephone	134
Do Take Muriel Out	136
The Weak Monk	137
Le Singe Qui Swing	138
The Broken Friendship	139

The After-thought   139
The Wanderer   140
No Categories!   141
The Deserter   142
I rode with my darling . . .   142
God and Man   143
Mr Over   144
My Cats   145
Drugs Made Pauline Vague   145
Our Bog is Dood   146
Wretched Woman   147
Lightly Bound   148
Le Revenant   148
To School!   148
To an American Publisher   149
The Rehearsal   149
Death-bed of a Financier   149
The Hat   149
The Ride   150
I Am   150
The Crown of Bays   151
A Jew is Angry with his Friend who does not
    Believe in Circumcision   153
From the Coptic   154
A Humane Materialist at the Burning of a
    Heretic   155
In Protocreation   155
Do Not!   156
The Death Sentence   157
The Commuted Sentence   157
The Celtic Fringe   158
The Leader   159
Oh, If Only . . .   160
Who Shot Eugenie?   160
Full Well I Know   162
Voices about the Princess Anemone   163
Deeply Morbid   163
The Ghost of Ware   166

Not Waving but Drowning	167
The English Visitor	168
'What is she writing? Perhaps it will be good'	169
The Fairy Bell	169
The New Age	170
The Blue from Heaven	171
The Lady of the Well-Spring	173
The Queen and the Young Princess	175
A Dream of Comparison	175
My Hat	176
The Engine Drain	177
Saint Anthony and the Rose of Life	180
Anger's Freeing Power	181
Fafnir and the Knights	182
Songe d'Athalie	184
The Hostage	185
Away, Melancholy	187
Dido's Farewell to Aeneas	189
Childe Rolandine	189
The Jungle Husband	190
'Come on, Come back'	191
Why are the Clergy . . .?	193
I Remember	193
But Murderous	194
This is Disgraceful and Abominable	194
God the Eater	196
God the Drinker	196
Will Man Ever Face Fact and not Feel Flat?	197
Every Lovely Limb's a Desolation	198
A Dream of Nourishment	199
The Airy Christ	200
It Filled my Heart with Love	201
I. An Agnostic	201
II. A Religious Man	202
Dear Little Sirmio	202
'Great Unaffected Vampires and the Moon'	203
The Celts	204
The Passing Cloud	205

Loin de l'Être   206
My Cat Major   207
Parents   208
To a Lady in a Train   209
Adelaide Abner   209
The English   210
King Hamlet's Ghost   211
At School   211
Can it Be?   214
The Old Sweet Dove of Wiveton   215
The Past   216
The Singing Cat   216
Longing for Death because of Feebleness   217
My Heart Goes Out   218
Look!   218
Who is this Who Howls and Mutters?   219
Magna est Veritas   220
The Light of Life   221
In the Park   221
Evangelie or The Figure of Literary Corruption,
    seeking Glory not Truth   223
Jumbo   223
The Choosers   224
The Occasional Yarrow   225
The Sorrowful Girl   225
The Starling   227
Die Lorelei   228
Farewell   229
Thoughts about the Person from Porlock   230
The Frog Prince   232
A House of Mercy   234
Avondale   235
Scorpion   236
Seymour and Chantelle or Un peu de vice   237
How do you see?   238
The Ass   243
A Soldier Dear to Us   246
The Forlorn Sea   249

Angel Boley   251
The Donkey   254
Cock-a-Doo   255
Francesca in Winter   256
So to fatness come   257
The Sallow Bird   258
The Word   258
Nor We of Her to Him   259
Mrs Blow and Her Animals   260
Oh grateful colours, bright looks!   262
O Pug!   263
Archie and Tina   264
The Poet Hin   266
The House of Over-Dew   268
The Galloping Cat   274
Hippy-Mo   276
Hendecasyllables   277
Black March   277
Grave by a Holm-Oak   279
The Sea-widow   280
The Stroke   281
Come, Death (II)   282

INDEX OF TITLES   283

INDEX OF FIRST LINES   287

PREFACE

STEVIE SMITH's first book, *Novel on Yellow Paper*, was published in 1936 when she was thirty-three. She had submitted a volume of poetry to Cape, the publishers, but they asked her to write a novel first and the poetry, *A Good Time Was Had By All*, followed the next year. Both were recognized for the original works they are, and her reputation grew slowly but steadily, rising to its peak at the time of her death at sixty-eight in 1971.

She was born in Hull, Yorkshire, and when she was three came with her mother and sister to live with her aunt in Palmers Green, London, eventually going to the North London Collegiate School for Girls, one of the late Victorian educational establishments that pioneered the idea that girls deserved as good a schooling as boys. She did not go to university and became a secretary in the magazine publishing company, Newnes, Pearson, where she continued to work until the early fifties, latterly as private secretary to Sir George Newnes and Sir Neville Pearson. She gave out that her work was never heavy. However, she did pick up good advice about investments and her estate showed that the advice must have been good, for her writing could not have made a major contribution to the reasonable sum she left.

She certainly seemed to have time to spare in her 'private office' to entertain her friends to tea and hot-buttered toast with strawberry jam – and conversation. I think her job amused her as the opening lines of *Novel on Yellow Paper* suggest: 'Beginning this book (not as they say "book" in our trade – they mean magazine) ...'

During all this period and until some ten years before her death, she lived with 'Aunt' (alone during all her maturity) and she ran the small house, a place of fascinatingly ugly décor, not a stick of which, as far as could be observed, had ever been changed since

Stevie's arrival, down to the aged gas cooker and a calendar with an *Art Nouveau* design that had only its date pad changed year after year. When her aunt became more or less bed-ridden, she gave up her office job to look after her – a duty she performed gladly. Her aunt, sometimes referred to as 'the Lion', was from the earliest days an important factor in Stevie's life. She was a sterling, capable character who supported Stevie and her elder sister, Molly, in every way and this was necessary, for their mother was not robust in health and their father often away. Stevie's health was never particularly good and from the age of five she spent the best part of three years in a home for tubercular children at Broadstairs. 'Aunt' is commemorated in her first novel: 'Darling Auntie Lion, I do so hope you will forgive what is written here. You are yourself like shining gold.'

Palmers Green was inconveniently placed in North London from the less unfashionable localities where her multitudes of friends lived and party-going was important but, somehow, she always got to them, either arranging for friends to drive her home or staying the night with her hostess. In this small way she was perhaps demanding but always rewarding – amused, amusing and deliciously barbed in her comments on people and events. She would arrive sometimes looking half-dead, hardly able to talk, yet within the time it took her to drink a glass of wine an astonishing transformation took place: she 'came alive' and would converse unflaggingly during the entire evening, the quality of her talk elusive as quicksilver and ranging from metaphysical speculation, through gossip, to raucous humour. Her will to live, this power of resurrection – not too strong a term though it would have touched off one of her wildest fantasies – was never more evident than on these occasions, and before going to her public engagements which she continued to keep till her illness was far advanced. Her description of her private audience with the Queen before the presentation of the 1969 Queen's Medal for Poetry may rank as one of her most vivid, wittiest stories; but one may be sure that her behaviour was highly and consciously professional, the more so for its spontaneity.

She was small-boned and frail-looking and dressed with some care in a style of her own which had, at first sight, and specially when she aged, a 'little girl' look; but one soon saw that it was perfectly appropriate and never without dignity. With her dark, straight, page-boy hair and dark eyes set in a pale, mobile face, she could have an almost sprite-like appearance. But in repose, and particularly in profile, her fine-boned features were of a striking beauty that was never more apparent than when death approached.

Novel on Yellow Paper and her third and last novel, *The Holiday*, reveal much of her character, apart from her religious beliefs. I am not qualified to define them but her life-long attachment to the Church of England, in belief and unbelief, is evident in her poetry, as it was in her conversation, even when she spoke or wrote vehemently against it and professed herself an unbeliever. An old friend, the Reverend Gerard Irvine has this to say:

In religion Stevie was ambivalent: neither a believer, an un-believer nor agnostic, but oddly all three at once. Intellectually she rejected the dogmas of her high Anglican background, as un-reasonable and morally inferior. But she had an obsessive concern with them. She demanded a maximizing faith to reject; she was scornful of what she considered watered-down reformulations of the faith, and disgusted by their liturgical expression. One could say that she did not like the God of Christian orthodoxy, but she could not disregard Him or ever quite bring herself to disbelieve in Him.

She did not believe, however, that suicide was necessarily wrong, and often discussed the possibility for herself, should life, mentally or physically, become intolerable. Indeed, death probably held less fear for her than most: she had come to terms with it as her 'gentle friend', in the manner of the metaphysical poets. Her last poem, *Come Death* (the second of that title), was written after she became fatally ill and, although she had lost her power of speech some weeks before her blessedly unprotracted death from brain tumour, she made it clear she did not wish her life to be pro-longed, handing me the typescript of that poem with the word 'death' encircled.

What I am sure gave her particular pleasure in the last decade of her life was the increasing demands made on her to give poetry readings, not just to societies but in schools. She had been acclaimed by the generation before her (the doyen of the London literary critics, Desmond MacCarthy, wrote 'she has a little nugget of genius'), by her contemporaries of course, and latterly, and more so than ever, by the new generation.

This new collection of Stevie Smith's poems has been selected from her complete poems, published in 1975. The choice is inevitably a subjective, even an arbitrary one, but my broad guidelines were to omit poems that were somewhat repetitive or unoriginal (in terms of a poet who was notably original) and the occasional trivia. It was an invidious task that was only undertaken to keep the length of the book within economic limits and in the knowledge that all her work is preserved in the collected poems. Inevitably many poems of merit and interest have had to be omitted from this edition, but perhaps it will direct readers to the complete collection.

Since 1977 her work has become familiar to many thousands, who might otherwise have missed it, through the success of Hugh Whitemore's play, *Stevie*, in which Glenda Jackson acted and spoke the poetry so brilliantly.

James MacGibbon

THE HOUND OF ULSTER

Little boy
Will you stop
And take a look
In the puppy shop –
Dogs blue and liver
Noses aquiver
Little dogs big dogs
Dogs for sport and pleasure
Fat dogs meagre dogs
Dogs for lap and leisure.
Do you see that wire-haired terrier?
Could anything be merrier?
Do you see that Labrador retriever?
His name is Belvoir.
    Thank you courteous stranger, said the child,
    By your words I am beguiled,
    But tell me I pray
    What lurks in the gray
    Cold shadows at the back of the shop?
Little boy do not stop
Come away
From the puppy shop.
For the Hound of Ulster lies tethered there
Cuchulain tethered by his golden hair
His eyes are closed and his lips are pale
Hurry little boy he is not for sale.

ON THE DEATH OF A GERMAN PHILOSOPHER

He wrote *The I and the It*
He wrote *The It and the Me*
He died at Marienbad
And now we are all at sea.

PAPA LOVE BABY

My mother was a romantic girl
So she had to marry a man with his hair in curl
Who subsequently became my unrespected papa,
But that was a long time ago now.

What folly it is that daughters are always supposed to be
In love with papa. It wasn't the case with me
I couldn't take to him at all
But he took to me
What a sad fate to befall
A child of three.

I sat upright in my baby carriage
And wished mama hadn't made such a foolish marriage.
I tried to hide it, but it showed in my eyes unfortunately
And a fortnight later papa ran away to sea.

He used to come home on leave
It was always the same
I could not grieve
But I think I was somewhat to blame.

BANDOL (VAR)

Bandol (Var)
In the south of France, my dear,
Is full of most awfully queer
Majors of the British Army, retired.

They live in boats tied up to the quay
(No income tax, no port dues here you see).

And they're always trying to buy or to sell each other things
And they hope what they lose on the roundabouts they'll
    make on the swings.

And they say
Quite in the best stage-army traditional way:
'England was quite a good place to live in before the War
Hawkahaw.'
They all seem to have got catarrh.

Bandol (Var)
How picturesque you are.

EGOCENTRIC

What care I if good God be
If he be not good to me,
If he will not hear my cry
Nor heed my melancholy midnight sigh?
What care I if he created Lamb,
And golden Lion, and mud-delighting Clam,
And Tiger stepping out on padded toe,
And the fecund earth the Blindworms know?

He made the Sun, the Moon and every Star,
He made the infant Owl and the Baboon,
He made the ruby-orbed Pelican,
He made all silent inhumanity,
Nescient and quiescent to his will,
Unquickened by the questing conscious flame
That is my glory and my bitter bane.
What care I if Skies are blue,
If God created Gnat and Gnu,
What care I if good God be
If he be not good to me?

ALFRED THE GREAT

Honour and magnify this man of men
Who keeps a wife and seven children on £2 10
Paid weekly in an envelope
And yet he never has abandoned hope.

MRS SIMPKINS

Mrs Simpkins never had very much to do
So it occurred to her one day that the Trinity wasn't true
Or at least but a garbled version of the truth
And that things had moved very far since the days of her youth.
So she became a spiritualist and at her very first party
Just to give her a feeling of confidence the spirit spoke up hearty:
'Since I crossed over dear friends' it said 'I'm no different to what
    I was before
Death's not a separation or alteration or parting it's just a
    one-handled door
We spirits can come back to you if your seance is orthodox
But you can't come over to us till your body's shut in a box
And this is the great thought I want to leave with you today
You've heard it before but in case you forgot death isn't a passing
    away
It's just a carrying on with friends relations and brightness
Only you don't have to bother with sickness and there's no
    financial tightness.'
Mrs Simpkins went home and told her husband he was a weak
    pated fellow
And when he heard the news he turned a daffodil shade of yellow
'What do you mean, Maria?' he cried, 'it can't be true there's no
    rest
From one's uncles and brothers and sisters nor even the wife of
    one's breast?'
'It's the truth,' Mrs Simpkins affirmed, 'there is no separation
There's a great reunion coming for which this life's but a
    preparation.'
This worked him to such a pitch that he shot himself through the
    head
And now she has to polish the floors of Westminster County Hall
    for her daily bread.

HOW FAR CAN YOU PRESS A POET?

How far can you press a poet?
To the last limit and he'll not show it
And one step further and he's dead
And his death is upon your head.

TO THE TUNE OF THE COVENTRY CAROL

The nearly right
And yet not quite
In love is wholly evil
And every heart
That loves in part
Is mortgaged to the devil.

I loved or thought
I loved in sort
Was this to love akin
To take the best
And leave the rest
And let the devil in?

O lovers true
And others too
Whose best is only better
Take my advice
Shun compromise
Forget him and forget her.

THE SUBURBAN CLASSES

There is far too much of the suburban classes
Spiritually not geographically speaking. They're asses.
Menacing the greatness of our beloved England, they lie
Propagating their kind in an eightroomed stye.
Now I have a plan which I will enfold
(There's this to be said for them, they do as they're told)
Then tell them their country's in mortal peril
They believed it before and again will not cavil
Put it in caption form firm and slick
If they see it in print it is bound to stick:
'Your King and your Country need you Dead'
You see the idea? Well, let it spread.
Have a suitable drug under string and label
Free for every Registered Reader's table.
For the rest of the gang who are not patriotic
I've another appeal they'll discover hypnotic:
Tell them it's smart to be dead and won't hurt
And they'll gobble up drug as they gobble up dirt.

SPANISH SCHOOL

The painters of Spain
Dipped their brushes in pain
By grief on a gallipot
Was Spanish tint begot.

Just see how Theotocopoulos
Throws on his canvas
Colours of hell
Christ lifts his head to cry
Once more I bleed and die
Mary emaciated cries:
Are men not satiated?

Must the blood of my son
For ever run?
The sky turns to burning oil
Blood red and yellow boil
Down from on high
Will no hills fall on us
To hide that sky?
Y Luciente's pen
Traces the life of men
Christs crucified upon a slope
They have no hope
Like Calderon who wrote in grief and scorn:
The greatest crime of man's to have been born.
Dr Péral
In a coat of gray
Has a way
With his mouth which seems to say
A lot
But nothing very good to hear
And as for Doña Ysabel Corbos de Porcel
Well
What a bitch
This seems to me a portrait which
Might have been left unhung
Or at anyrate slung
A little higher up.

But never mind there's always Ribera
With his little lamb
(Number two-four-four)
To give a more
Genial atmosphere
And a little jam
For the pill –
But still.

NIGHT-TIME IN THE CEMETERY

The funeral paths are hung with snow
About the graves the mourners go
To think of those who lie below.
The churchyard pales are black against the night
And snow hung here seems doubly white.
I have a horror of this place
A horror of each moonlit mourner's face
These people are not familiar
But strange and stranger than strange peculiar
They have that look of a cheese do you know sour-sweet
You can smell their feet.
Yet must I tread
About my dead
And guess the forms within the grave
And hear the clank of jowl on jowl
Where low lie kin no love could save.
Yet stand I by my grave as they by theirs. Oh bitter Death
That brought their love and mine unto a coffin's breadth.

ALONE IN THE WOODS

Alone in the woods I felt
The bitter hostility of the sky and the trees
Nature has taught her creatures to hate
Man that fusses and fumes
Unquiet man
As the sap rises in the trees
As the sap paints the trees a violent green

So rises the wrath of Nature's creatures
At man
So paints the face of Nature a violent green.
Nature is sick at man
Sick at his fuss and fume
Sick at his agonies
Sick at his gaudy mind
That drives his body
Ever more quickly
More and more
In the wrong direction.

GOD AND THE DEVIL

God and the Devil
Were talking one day
Ages and ages of years ago.
God said: Suppose
Things were fashioned this way,
Well then, so and so.
The Devil said: No,
Prove it if you can.
So God created Man
And that is how it all began.
It has continued now for many a year
And sometimes it seems more than we can bear.
But why should bowels yearn and cheeks grow pale?
We're here to point a moral and adorn a tale.

ES WAR EINMAL

I raised my gun
I took the sight
Against the sun
I shot a kite.

    I raised my gun
    I took the sight
    A second one
    I shot in flight.

        I raised my gun
        I shot a plover
        I loaded up
        And shot another.

            Now round about me
            Lay the dead
            One more, one more,
            Then home to bed.

Pray Heaven, said I
Send the best
That ever took
Lead to its breast.

    Upon the word
    Upon the right
    Rose up a phoenix
    Beaming bright.

        I raised my gun
        I took the sight
        My lead unbarred
        That breast of white,

Alas for awful
Magic art
The bullet bounced
Into my heart.

The phoenix bled
My heart can not
But heavy sits
Neath leaden shot.

Leave shooting, friend,
Or if you must
Shoot only what
Is mortal dust.

Pray not to Heaven
He stock your bag
Or you may feel
Your vitals sag.

Pray not to Heaven
For heavenly bird
Or Heaven may take you
At your word.

NUMBERS

A thousand and fifty-one waves
Two hundred and thirty-one seagulls
A cliff of four hundred feet
Three miles of ploughed fields
One house
Four windows look on the waves

Four windows look on the ploughed fields
One skylight looks on the sky
In that skylight's sky is one seagull.

FROM THE COUNTY LUNATIC ASYLUM

The people say that spiritism is a joke and a swizz,
The Church that it is dangerous – not half it is.

THE BEREAVED SWAN

Wan
Swan
On the lake
Like a cake
Of soap
Why is the swan
Wan
On the lake?
He has abandoned hope.

Wan
Swan
On the lake afloat
Bows his head:
O would that I were dead
For her sake that lies
Wrapped from my eyes
In a mantle of death,
The swan saith.

CORRESPONDENCE BETWEEN MR HARRISON IN NEWCASTLE AND MR SHOLTO PEACH HARRISON IN HULL

Sholto Peach Harrison you are no son of mine
And do you think I bred you up to cross the River Tyne
And do you think I bred you up (and mother says the same)
And do you think I bred you up to live a life of shame
To live a life of shame my boy as you are thinking to
Down south in Kingston-upon-Hull a traveller in glue?
Come back my bonny boy nor break your father's heart
Come back and marry Lady Susan Smart
She has a mint in Anglo-Persian oil
And Sholto never more need think of toil.

You are an old and evil man my father
I tell you frankly Sholto had much rather
Travel in glue unrecompensed unwed
Than go to church with oily Sue and afterwards to bed.

NATURE AND FREE ANIMALS

I will forgive you everything,
But what you have done to my Dogs
I will not forgive.
You have taught them the sicknesses of your mind
And the sicknesses of your body
You have taught them to be servile
To hang servilely upon your countenance
To be dependent touching and entertaining
To have rights to be wronged
And wrongs to be righted.
You have taught them to be protected by a Society.
This I will not forgive,
Saith the Lord.
Well, God, it's all very well to talk like this
And I dare say it's all very fine
And Nature and Free Animals
Are all very fine,
Well all I can say is
If you wanted it like that
You shouldn't have created me
Not that I like it very much
And now that I'm on the subject I'll say,
What with Nature and Free Animals on the one side
And you on the other,
I hardly know I'm alive.

ENG.

What has happened to the young men of Eng.?
Why are they so lovey-dovey so sad and so domesticated
So sad and so philoprogenitive

So sad and without sensuality?
They love with a ci-devant feminine affection
They see in their dreams a little home
And *kiddies*
Ah the *kiddies*
They would not mind *having* babies:
It is unkind
Of Nature to lag behind.

DEATH BEREAVES OUR COMMON MOTHER NATURE GRIEVES FOR MY DEAD BROTHER

Lamb dead, dead lamb,
He was, I am,
Separation by a tense
Baulks my eyes' indifference.
Can I see the lately dead
And not bend a sympathetic head?
Can I see lamb dead as mutton
And not care a solitary button?

BAG-SNATCHING IN DUBLIN

Sisley
Walked so nicely
With footsteps so discreet
To see her pass
You'd never guess
She walked upon the street.

Down where the Liffy waters' turgid flood
Churns up to greet the ocean-driven mud,
A bruiser in a fix
Murdered her for 6/6.

THE RIVER DEBEN

All the waters of the river Deben
Go over my head to the last wave even
Such a death were sweet to seven times seven.

Death sits in the boat with me
His face is shrouded but he smiles I see
The time is not yet, he will not come so readily.

But he smiles and I smile it is pleasant in the boat at night
There is no moon rising but from the east a light
Shines in the sky, is it dawn or dawn's twilight?

Over here the waters are dark as a deep chasm
Shadowed by cliffs of volcanic spasm
So dark so dark is the waves' fashion.

But the oars dip I am rowing they dip and scatter
The phosphorescence in a sudden spatter
Of light that is more actual than a piece of matter.

Up the Deben we row I row towards Waldringfield
It is a long way yet, my arms ache but will not yield
In this physical tiredness there is a happy shield.

Oh happy Deben, oh happy night, and night's companion Death,
What exultation what ecstasy is in thy breath
It is as salt as the salt silt that lies beneath.

Flow tidal river flow, draw wind from the east,
Smile pleasant Death, smile Death in darkness blessed,
But tarry day upon the crack of dawn. Thou comest unwished.

DEATH CAME TO ME

Death came to me and said
'Which will you choose?
'Use one
'Or all of these to summon me.
'I'll come.'
And with a smile he'd gone.
There lay a knife
A labelled flask a gun.

I took the knife
Its cruel edge would bite
Into my flesh
Had I the resolution or the art
To bear the smart
And drive it to my heart?
Not I. I say
I love my flesh too much
For such
A way.

I took the flask and turned the label up –
Eastern Syrop – what a stirrup cup
For my short ride into eternity
And what a shame
To give a lordly drug so base a name
That better than this bottleful
Had decked a novelette by Mrs Hull.

For underneath the superscription lurked I knew
With pulses quickening and the blood thickening
For fear in every vein the deadly strychnine
It paralysed the heart at once they said, but I
Had not the heart to try.

I took the revolver in my hand and broke it open.
A Webley, service pattern, is a useful weapon
I liked it for the magazine chock-full
Of ammunition, liked the dull
Shimmer of its barrel in the firelight's glimmer.
It had an air of quiet distinction lying there.
The handmaid of extinction
Had killed a better man than I had ever been
In nineteen hundred and fourteen.*
I snapped it to,
It weighed about a ton,
And two
Were on the trigger
Phew
I put it to my head
And now I'm dead.

NO RESPECT

I have no respect for you
For you would not tell the truth about your grief
But laughed at it
When the first pang was past
And made it a thing of nothing.
You said

* This and the preceding line were marked for deletion in the author's
own copy.

That what had been
Had never been
That what was
Was not:
You have a light mind
And a coward's soul.

THE REASON

My life is vile
I hate it so
I'll wait awhile
And then I'll go.

Why wait at all?
Hope springs alive,
Good may befall
I yet may thrive.

It is because I can't make up my mind
If God is good, impotent or unkind.

I LIKE TO PLAY WITH HIM

I like to play with him
He would be lovely to play with
He is so solemn sensitive conceited
He would be lovely to play with
I could pretend
Say so-and-so and so-and-so
Watch his responses

How'd he take that today
And this tomorrow,
Mood, tense, you see
I'd conjugate His Inexcellency.

Oh on that evening you were
So charming enchanting touching
Lost wounded and betrayed
Oh that should have been only the beginning.

ANALYSAND

He chases his tail
Like a puppy-fool
And wonders it tastes stale
The puppy-fool.

All thoughts that are turned inward to their source
Bring one to self-hatred and remorse
The punishment is suicide of course.

But first he'll tread
A calvary
From bed to bed
Of misery

And lying thinking on his bed of stone
No sleep will come to him he is alone
For evermore with every aching bone.

His spirit flags
His body slumps
His spirit nags
His mental dumps.

Self dedicated to self scrutiny
His every moment's an eternity
Of irritation and monotony.

For fuss and fret
His tears fall down
His brow is set
In savage frown.

But is it surprising Reader do you think?
Would you expect to find him in the pink
Who's solely occupied with his own mental stink?

SUNT LEONES

The lions who ate the Christians on the sands of the arena
By indulging native appetites played what has now been seen a
Not entirely negligible part
In consolidating at the very start
The position of the Early Christian Church.
Initiatory rites are always bloody
And the lions, it appears
From contemporary art, made a study
Of dyeing Coliseum sands a ruddy
Liturgically sacrificial hue
And if the Christians felt a little blue –
Well people being eaten often do.
Theirs was the death, and theirs the crown undying,
A state of things which must be satisfying.
My point which up to this has been obscured
Is that it was the lions who procured

By chewing up blood gristle flesh and bone
The martyrdoms on which the Church has grown.
I only write this poem because I thought it rather looked
As if the part the lions played was being overlooked.
By lions' jaws great benefits and blessings were begotten
And so our debt to Lionhood must never be forgotten.

LORD MOPE

What shall we say of this curious young man?
Scion of aristocracy sycophant of eld
Sitting at the feet of the old men because they are old
Warming his shivering behind at their gutted flame . . .
Brace up oh bunny heart, that man's no sage
Though the years heap on his head, be not deceived.
Each year is but a weight
To sky his empty pate
Nearer to heaven's gate
Nearer his god to him
(His god of prejudice and whim).
Oh fearful young man shivering ridiculously
What shall I say to give you heart oh poor young man?
No shield is in the old
Better to be young and cold
(Shivering ridiculously in your four-and-twenty years)
Better to be young, a Cry-baby, a Pet,
Than to be an old man, mouthing in a fret.
Better to be young and let the cold tears fall and ravage
Than to be an Old Boy, senile, simian and savage.

NEVER AGAIN

Never again will I weep
And wring my hands
And beat my head against the wall
Because
Me nolentem fata trahunt
But
When I have had enough
I will arise
And go unto my Father
And I will say to Him:
Father, I have had enough.

LITTLE BOY LOST

The wood was rather old and dark
The witch was very ugly
And if it hadn't been for father
Walking there so smugly
I never should have followed
The beckoning of her finger.
Ah me how long ago it was
And still I linger
Under the ever interlacing beeches
Over a carpet of moss
I lift my hand but it never reaches
To where the breezes toss
The sun-kissed leaves above.
The sun?
Beware.
The sun never comes here.
Round about and round I go
Up and down and to and fro

The woodlouse hops upon the tree
Or should do but I really cannot see.
Happy fellow. Why can't I be
Happy as he?
The wood grows darker every day
It's not a bad place in a way
But I lost the way
Last Tuesday
Did I love father, mother, home?
Not very much; but now they're gone
I think of them with kindly toleration
Bred inevitably of separation.
Really if I could find some food
I should be happy enough in this wood
But darker days and hungrier I must spend
Till hunger and darkness make an end.

ANGEL OF GRACE

I was talking one day
To a lady gay
When my Guardian Angel
Plucked me away:
Where can she be
Oh where does she wander
That lady of whom
I grow fonder and fonder?

FREDDY

Nobody knows what I feel about Freddy
I cannot make anyone understand
I love him sub specie aeternitatis
I love him out of hand.
I don't love him so much in the restaurants that's a fact
To get him hobnob with my old pub chums needs too much tact
He don't love them and they don't love him
In the pub lub lights they say Freddy very dim.
But get him alone on the open saltings
Where the sea licks up to the fen
He is his and my own heart's best
World without end ahem.
People who say we ought to get married ought to get smacked:
Why should we do it when we can't afford it and have ourselves
    whacked?
Thank you kind friends and relations thank *you*,
We do very well as we do.
Oh what do I care for the pub lub lights
And the friends I love so well –
There's more in the way I feel about Freddy
Than a friend can tell.
But all the same I don't care much for his meelyoo I mean
I don't anheimate mich in the ha-ha well-off suburban scene
Where men are few and hearts go tumptytum
In the tennis club lub lights poet very dumb.
But there never was a boy like Freddy
For a haystack's ivory tower of bliss
Where speaking sub specie humanitatis
Freddy and me can kiss.
Exiled from his meelyoo
Exiled from mine
There's all Tom Tiddler's time pocket
For his love and mine.

IS IT WISE?

Is it wise
To hug misery
To make a song of Melancholy
To weave a garland of sighs
To abandon hope wholly?
No, it is not wise.

Is it wise
To love Mortality
To make a song of Corruptibility
A chain of linked lies
To bind Mutability?
No, it is not wise.

Is it wise
To endure
To call up Old Fury
And Pain for a martyr's dowry
When Death's a prize
Easy to carry?
No, it is not wise.

THIS ENGLISHWOMAN

This Englishwoman is so refined
She has no bosom and no behind.

LORD BARRENSTOCK

Lord Barrenstock and Epicene,
What's it to me that you have been
In your pursuit of interdicted joys
Seducer of a hundred little boys?

Your sins are red about your head
And many people wish you dead.

You trod the widow in the mire
Wronged the son, deceived the sire.

You put a fence about the land
And made the people's cattle graze on sand.

Ratted from many a pool and forced amalgamation
And dealt in shares which never had a stock exchange quotation.

Non flocci facio, I do not care
For wrongs you made the other fellow bear:
'Tis not for these unsocial acts not these
I wet my pen. I would not have you tease,
With a repentance smug and overdue
For all the things you still desire to do,
The ears of an outraged divinity:
But oh your tie is crooked and I see
Too plain you had an éclair for your tea.

It is this nonchalance about your person –
That is the root of my profound aversion.

You are too fat. In spite of stays
Your shape is painful to the polished gaze;
Your uncombed hair grows thin and daily thinner,
In fact you're far too ugly to be such a sinner.

Lord Barrenstock and Epicene, consider all that you have done
Lord Epicene and Barrenstock, yet not two Lords but one,
I think you are an object not of fear but pity
Be good, my Lord, since you can not be pretty.

MAXIMILIAN ESTERHAZY

O Maximilian stern and wild
Wilt thou not look on me thy little child
Thy once so darling dear, so closely presst,
So cared for, so extravagantly dresst,
Raised up from nothing in thy thought to be
A furnished dwelling of felicity?
Now thou dost frown and all my walls descend
Like Jericho's and there is a swift end
Of comely donjon and of crested tops
Of flying buttresses and decorated props.
O never castle in the hills of Spain
Was half so much of nothing as thy Jane,
When thou dost turn away and no more look,
She is a song unsung, an unwrit book.

MAJOR MACROO

Major Hawkaby Cole Macroo
Chose
Very wisely
A patient Griselda of a wife with a heart of gold
That never beat for a soul but him
Himself and his slightest whim.

He left her alone for months at a time
When he had to have a change
Just had to
And his pension wouldn't stretch to a fare for two
And he didn't want it to.

And if she wept she was game and nobody knew it
And she stood at the edge of the tunnel and waved as his train
    went through it.

And because it was cheaper they lived abroad
And did he care if she might be unhappy or bored?
He did not.
He'd other things to think of – a lot.

He'd fads and he fed them fat,
And she could lump it and that was that.

He'd several boy friends
And she thought it was nice for him to have them,
And she loved him and felt that he needed her and waited
And waited and never became exasperated.

Even his room
Was dusted and kept the same,
And when friends came
They went into every room in the house but that one
Which Hawkaby wouldn't have shown.

Such men as these, such selfish cruel men
Hurting what most they love what most loves them,
Never make a mistake when it comes to choosing a woman
To cherish them and be neglected and not think it inhuman.

PRIVATE MEANS IS DEAD
(Originally entitled Chaps)

Private Means is dead
God rest his soul, officers and fellow-rankers said.
Captive Good, attending Captain Ill
Can tell us quite a lot about the Captain, if he will.

Major Portion
Is a disingenuous person
And as for Major Operation well I guess
We all know what his reputation is.

The crux and Colonel
Of the whole matter
(As you may read in the Journal
If it's not tattered)

Lies in the Generals Collapse Debility Panic and Uproar
Who are too old in any case to go to the War.

BEREAVEMENT

Maria Holt
Was not the dolt
That people thought her.
Her face was full
Her mind not dull
She was my daughter.
She had so much to do so very much
And used to shuffle round upon a crutch,
The younger children always called her mother,
And so she was to sister and to brother
Poor wretch she's dead and now I am bereft
Of £60 each year to fill the place she left
I never paid a cent before; it is too bad,
It's worse to lose a lass than lose a lad.

DEATH OF MR MOUNSEL

I am dying Egypt dying
Keep my watch and send word home
Never mind about the funeral
Just a simple coping stone
Manly virtue needs no bushel
Baby hands that cling and tear
Better twenty years of Kathy
Than the fiend's own heart of fear
Solitude corrupting manners
Often has the tale been told
Memory paints a brighter pansy
Springing from the funeral mould
Let my grave with wrath no stranger
Visit nor complaining come
Unmolested quit of danger
Quietly I slip hence and home
But when lights are glowing lower
Pressing downward through the gloom
And the porter shows the lady
To the first-class waiting-room
Then let every City Pretty –
You not least dear you not least –
Shed a tear for Mister Mounsel
Most unhappily deceased.

WHO KILLED LAWLESS LEAN?

The parrot
Is eating a carrot
In his cage in the garret

Why is the parrot's
Cage in the garret?
He is not a sage
Parrot: his words enrage.

Downstairs
In his bed
Lies the head
Of the family
He is dead.

And the brothers gather
Mutter utter would rather
Forget
The words the parrot
Said.

When high in his cage swinging
From the lofty ceiling
Sat the pet screaming:
'Who killed Lawless Lean?'
It was not at all fitting.

So they put the parrot
In his cage in the garret
And gave him a carrot
To keep him quiet.
He should be glad they did not wring his neck.

ROAD UP

It seemed a curious place to rest one's body and take one's ease
Here in the very middle of Euston Road.
Now if it had been on the Thames' green bank, under poplar trees,
But here the traffic instead of the water flowed.

It was a British working man who lay full length on his back
And every now and then he turned and hit the road a thwack.
Was he dowser tapping for water I wonder,
Or was it a sudden spasm of rage that split his dreams asunder?

MRS OSMOSIS

Mrs Osmosis
Is all right in small doses
Like what I was saying about Mrs Pale
There's a tell-tale
And for why?
Cos I blacked her eye
Last Fri—
day.
It don't sound natural to me
But they do say Mr P.
Well it all comes of her going with a fellow which ain't hardly so
    to say
Not that *he'd* cause to worry, seeing it was that way.

THE FUGITIVE'S RIDE

Across the bridge across the dyke
Foresworn by friend and foe alike,
I ride
The field upon the further side
Stretches before me and its wide

Horizon dark against dark sky
Beckons me on. Dim homesteads lie
To left and right as I ride by.

It is a wet and steamy night,
More steamy night I have not seen,
More steamy night there has not been,
I have rode on for many a mile
And now it does not rain
And has not done for quite a while
And all the plain
Lies limpid underneath the stars
That give an eerie light
And make the plain seem to be bright.
With standing water, deep or shallow?
Deep lake, or river? Corn or fallow?
Lord, Lord, I cannot say
But warily I pick my way
This false starlight is worse than no light
To bewitch
The eyes and hide the gaping ditch.

What owl was that that howls upon
The trees athwart the stream
And have I been this way before
Or do I dream?
He seems to be a mournful one
That hoots to make a coward run
I hate to hear I hate to see
An owl that hoots so dismally
It makes my very blood run cold
No bird should dare to be so bold
I feel as fearful as he should
Who's done a dreadful deed of blood.

(Now hold up horse a moment pray,
Don't sidestep in that foolish way,
If you fall down upon the ground
There is a chance you will be drowned.)

A wetter plain I have not seen
A wetter plain there has not been
I say there has not been
A wetter plain
Since first I came
And may I die
If once again it does not rain.
In early dawn is this dark plain
Made darker still of darkness shorn
More dismaller but still the same
Lit by the ray that heralds day.

On my poor horse so lost so wan
That cannot understand
Why we must ride and ride and ride
And never yet come home
On you must go until you drop
For since time won't, I dare not stop.

SUBURB

How nice it is to slink the streets at night
And taste the slight
Flavour of acrity that comes
From pavements throwing off the dross
Of human tread.
Each paving stone sardonic
Grins to its fellow citizen masonic:

'Thank God they're gone,' each to the other cries
'Now there is nothing between us and the skies'.
Joy at this state transports the hanging heavens
And down to earth they rain celestial dew
The pavement darkly gleams beneath the lamp
Forgetful now of daylight's weary tramp.
Round about the streets I slink
Suburbs are not so bad I think
When their inhabitants can not be seen,
Even Palmers Green.
Nobody loves the hissing rain as I
And round about I slink
And presently
Turn from the sleek wet pavements to the utter slime
Where jerrybuilders building against time
Pursue their storied way,
Foundations and a pram,
Four walls and a pot of jam,
They have their sentries now
Upon a hundred hillocks.
Night watchman bad and old
Take rheumatism in exchange for gold.
Do you see that pub between the trees
Which advertises gin and cyclists' teas?
Down there I know a lane
Under the padding rain
Where leaves are born again
Every night
And reach maturity
In a remote futurity
Before dawn's light.
I have never seen
Anything quite so green
So close so dark so bright
As the green leaves at night.

I will not show you yet
Lest you should forget,
But when the time is come for your dismembering
I'll show you that you may die remembering.

BEWARE THE MAN

Beware the man whose mouth is small
For he'll give nothing and take all.

BREUGHEL

The ages blaspheme
The people are weak
As in a dream
They evilly speak.

Their words in a clatter
Of meaningless sound
Without form or matter
Echo around.

The people oh Lord
Are sinful and sad
Prenatally biassed
Grow worser born bad

They sicken oh Lord
They have no strength in them
Oh rouse up my God
And against their will win them.

Must thy lambs to the slaughter
Delivered be
With each son and daughter
Irrevocably?

From tower and steeple
Ring out funeral bells
Oh Lord save thy people
They have no help else.

TENDER ONLY TO ONE

Tender only to one
Tender and true
The petals swing
To my fingering
Is it you, or you, or you?

Tender only to one
I do not know his name
And the friends who fall
To the petals' call
May think my love to blame.

Tender only to one
This petal holds a clue
The face it shows
But too well knows
Who I am tender to.

Tender only to one,
Last petal's latest breath
Cries out aloud
From the icy shroud
His name, his name is Death.

O HAPPY DOGS OF ENGLAND

O happy dogs of England
Bark well as well you may
If you lived anywhere else
You would not be so gay.

O happy dogs of England
Bark well at errand boys
If you lived anywhere else
You would not be allowed to make such an infernal noise.

DARLING DAUGHTERS

Darling daughters, listen to your mother,
I must go away and leave you to each other,
And one shall marry a rich man
And one shall go on an excursion to the Isle of Man
And one shall find her way home if she can.

THE BISHOPS OF THE
CHURCH OF ENGLAND

I admire the Bishops of the Church of England
No man can be a Bishop of the Church of England
And a fool.
A man can be a Bishop of the Church of England
And a knave.
But
Fortunately
Few if any of the Bishops of the Church of England
Are men of ill will.
They do their best
To resolve wisely
To govern effectively.
They are the butt of the ignoramus,
Of the sentimentalist,
Of the man who makes

Of his own bad temper and incompetency
A Movement for the Amelioration of the Sufferings
Of the Oppressed Members of the Lower Middle Classes.

EULENSPIEGELEI

To be so cold and yet not old
Oh what can ail the changeling child?
She has an eye that is too bold
Upon the night. She is beguiled.

The night is dark and the windowpane
Holds the rattle of the falling rain.
Oh look not forth but look within
Where the room lies safe from the stormwinds' din.

The tears upon the infant eyes
Are held in icy thrall
And when she speaks contrariwise
The riven echoes fall:

Oh mother come not near me now
Nor lay thy hand on my cold cold brow
Few years if any heap on my head
But I am old as the newly dead.

Now louder far than the stormwinds' jar
And the voice of mother and child
Is heard the scritch of the gravid bitch
That will be so wild.

Oh what can ail the gravid bitch
That howls upon the midnight stroke?
Dear mother dear I cannot say
Perhaps the devil gave her a poke.

The changeling child from her bed is gone
The mother weeps alone
And the stormwinds beat on the window pane
To mock the maternal moan.

Oh whither is fled thy changeling child
And by what witching craft?
It was the Eulenspiegel spake
And as he spake he laughed.

For well he knew that wrought it so,
The bitch and the changeling too
Are vanished away from the stormwinds' play
And the stricken mother's mew.

THE ABOMINABLE LAKE

Deep in the still mysterious waters of the lake a world lies
    drowned.
How sombre and sad the silent world in the womb of the lake,
Not the reflection of Tellus, not the arch of heaven
Lies in the waters of the abominable lake,
But an earth and a heaven beyond the dominion of Time,
Beyond the soft sensual touch of the seasonal flow
And the inviolable sequence of midnight and noon.
Poor world, my heart breaks for your sealed inarticulate woe,
And the tears that are frozen in yours melt to flood in my eyes,
Overflow and descend and impinge on the waters of the lake
And shatter at once the form of the silent world.
But the teardrops mingle, the waters shudder and close,
And again and again the sad world is revealed to my sight.

Then I know, and the knowledge transfixes my sensitive heart,
Not my tears, nor my prayers, nor my gold shall encompass at last
A freedom unthought, manumission unhoped, undesired.

ONE OF MANY

You are only one of many
And of small account if any,
You think about yourself too much.
This touched the child with a quick touch
And worked his mind to such a pitch
He threw his fellows in a ditch.
This little child
That was so mild
Is grown too wild.

Murder in the first degree, cried Old Fury,
Recording the verdict of the jury.

Now they are come to the execution tree.
The gallows stand wide. Ah me, ah me.

Christ died for sinners, intoned the Prison Chaplain from his
        miscellany.
Weeping bitterly the little child cries: I die one of many.

DEATH'S OSTRACISM

He trod in dream upon the brim
Of a deep sea, his mirth too young for him,
For all the people that he smiled upon
Cry: Fool. And they are gone.

With what hostility
And pride
They saw and fled.
He sighed.

The sea ran heavy on a core
Of hidden deep disturbance, ah before
The dream came had an earthquake first
The seabed burst.

Now from the depths
He sees
The sullied water rise.
All is disease.

And the long reaching waves swing wide,
Sick with death's taste upon the flooding tide,
And dead sea monsters with a deep appal
Of open wounds upon the water sprawl.

His foothold slips.
The clay
Rank with long rains
Gives way.

But falling he will call the waves to friend,
Come cover over all and make an end.
No use, they will not do it, they swing aside.
Death's ostracism in a dream he must abide.

THE BOAT

The boat that took my love away
He sent again to me
To tell me that he should not sleep
Alone beneath the sea.

The flower and fruit of love are mine
The ant, the fieldmouse and the mole,
But now a tiger prowls without
And claws upon my soul.

Love is not love that wounded bleeds
And bleeding sullies slow.
Come death within my hands and I
Unto my love will go.

PARROT

The old sick green parrot
High in a dingy cage
Sick with malevolent rage
Beadily glutted his furious eye
On the old dark
Chimneys of Noel Park

Far from his jungle green
Over the seas he came
To the yellow skies, to the dripping rain,
To the night of his despair.
And the pavements of his street
Are shining beneath the lamp
With a beauty that's not for one
Born under a tropic sun.

He has croup. His feathered chest
Knows no minute of rest.
High on his perch he sits
And coughs and spits,
Waiting for death to come.
Pray heaven it wont be long.

THE DOCTOR

You are not looking at all well, my dear,
In fact you are looking most awfully queer.
Do you find that the pain is more than you can bear?

Yes, I find that it is more than I can bear, so give me some bromide
And then I will go away for a long time and hide
Somewhere on the seashore where the tide

Coming upon me when I am asleep shall cover
Me, go over entirely,
Carry beyond recovery.

I HATE THIS GIRL

I hate this girl
She is so cold.
And yet her eyes say
She is not so good as gold.
I should like to kill her,
But what do I do?
Kiss her, kiss her,
And wish that she would kiss me too.

INFELICE

Walking swiftly with a dreadful duchess,
He smiled too briefly, his face was as pale as sand,
He jumped into a taxi when he saw me coming,
Leaving me alone with a private meaning,
He loves me so much, my heart is singing.
Later at the Club when I rang him in the evening
They said: Sir Rat is dining, is dining, is dining,
No Madam, he left no message, ah how his silence speaks,
He loves me too much for words, my heart is singing.
The Pullman seats are here, the tickets for Paris, I am waiting,
Presently the telephone rings, it is his valet speaking,
Sir Rat is called away, to Scotland, his constituents,
(Ah the dreadful duchess, but he loves me best)
Best pleasure to the last, my heart is singing.
One night he came, it was four in the morning,
Walking slowly upstairs, he stands beside my bed,
Dear darling, lie beside me, it is too cold to stand speaking,
He lies down beside me, his face is like the sand,
He is in a sleep of love, my heart is singing.
Sleeping softly softly, in the morning I must wake him,
And waking he murmurs, I only came to sleep.
The words are so sweetly cruel, how deeply he loves me,
I say them to myself alone, my heart is singing.
Now the sunshine strengthens, it is ten in the morning,
He is so timid in love, he only needs to know,
He is my little child, how can he come if I do not call him,
I will write and tell him everything, I take the pen and write:
I love you so much, my heart is singing.

Why dost thou dally, Death, and tarry on the way?
When I have summoned thee with prayers and tears, why dost
    thou stay?
Come, Death, and carry now my soul away.

Wilt thou not come for calling, must I show
Force to constrain thy quick attention to my woe?
I have a hand upon thy Coat, and will
Not let thee go.

How foolish are the words of the old monks,
In Life remember Death.
Who would forget
Thou closer hangst on every finished breath?
How vain the work of Christianity
To teach humanity
Courage in its mortality.
Who would not rather die
And quiet lie
Beneath the sod
With or without a god?

Foolish illusion, what has Life to give?
Why should man more fear Death than fear to live?

SILENCE AND TEARS

A priestly garment, eminently suitable for conducting funeral services in inclement weather.

From a church outfitter's catalogue

The tears of the widow of the military man
Fell down to the earth as the funeral sentence ran.
Dust to dust, Oh how frightful sighed the mourners as the rain
    began.

But the grave yawned wide and took the tears and the rain,
And the poor dead man was at last free from all his pain,
Pee-wee sang the little bird upon the tree again and again.

Is it not a solemn moment when the last word is said,
And wrapped in cloak of priestly custom we dispose our dead,
And the earth falls heavy, heavy, upon the expensive coffin lined
    with lead?

And may the coffin hold his bones in peace that lies below,
And may the widow woman's tears make a good show,
And may the suitable priestly garment not let the breath of scandal
    through.

For the weather of their happening has been a little inclement,
And would people be so sympathetic if they knew how the story
    went?
Best not put it to the test. Silence and tears are convenient.

A FATHER FOR A FOOL

To the tune 'Boys and Girls Come out to Play'.

Little Master Home-from-School,
This is the Parkland you must rule.
What does it feel like to have a father for a fool?
Your father mortgaged the estate,
Lost his money, blamed fate
And shot himself through the head too late.
There's a father for a fool,
My little Master Home-from-School.

Why does Auntie wear such funny hats
And invert her sentences? Now that's
Positive proof she must be bats.
Why has Parker got all the horses out for me?
Why doesn't Ma meet the train as usually?
Here's hoping they give us shrimps for tea.

Little Master Home-from-School,
Your Ma lies dead, she lies too cool,
She's stone cold dead of a broken heart, the fool.
Jingle-jog the horses go,
And Parker's thinking what I know:
Here comes Master Home-from-School
That had a father for a fool.

BRICKENDEN, HERTFORDSHIRE

Sitting alone of a summer's evening,
I thought
Of the tragedy of unwatered country.

O little village of Brickenden,
Where is thy stream,
Translucent drain of thy manorial sward?
Thy sward is green,
Its source of verdancy guessed but unseen.
Where is thy stream?
I have beat every bound of this wild wood.
I have trod down its spiteful and detaining undergrowth,
Seeking a broad stream and contented fish,
Seeking but finding not.
Now that the sun
Sou'westering in the sky
Tells me that evening is come,
I rest
Oppressed
By the wood's profligate viridity,
By thy wood's sap,
Child of a moisture that I cannot tap.

O woods of Brickenden, you have confounded me
By your appearance of humidity.
I see the pashy ground,
And round and round
My tired feet the rushes twine,
And frogs croak and the sweating slime
Is moved about by an ambiguous brood
Of low and legless life.
Hadst thou thy stream,
O wood of Brickenden,
This had been
Paradise.

But thy sap's virtue comes from dank earth's sweat,
And to be wet
Is not enough, O wood.

Hadst thou thy stream,
O little village of Brickenden,
Thy stream
Had salined thee
By virtue of destinatory sea,
And thou hadst been
A Paradise.
But lacking stream
Art but a suppuration of earth's humours.
Sitting alone on a summer's evening,
I wept
For the tragedy of unwatered country.
Take thou my tears, O Brickenden,
They are thy rank sweat's sea.

THE MURDERER

My true love breathed her latest breath
And I have closed her eyes in death.
It was a cold and windy day
In March, when my love went away.
She was not like other girls – rather diffident,
And that is how we had an accident.

MOTHER, AMONG THE DUSTBINS

Mother, among the dustbins and the manure
I feel the measure of my humanity, an allure
As of the presence of God. I am sure

In the dustbins, in the manure, in the cat at play,
Is the presence of God, in a sure way
He moves there. Mother, what do you say?

I too have felt the presence of God in the broom
I hold, in the cobwebs in the room,
But most of all in the silence of the tomb.

Ah! but that thought that informs the hope of our kind
Is but an empty thing, what lies behind? –
Naught but the vanity of a protesting mind

That would not die. This is the thought that bounces
Within a conceited head and trounces
Inquiry. Man is most frivolous when he pronounces.

Well Mother, I shall continue to feel as I do,
And I think you would be wise to do so too,
Can you question the folly of man in the creation of God?
    Who are you?

LE DÉSERT DE L'AMOUR

I want to be your pinkie
I am tender to you
My heart opens like a cactus flower
Do you thinky I will do?

My heart is like a cactus
Not like a cactus flower
And I can kill love
Without entering her bower.

So they both thought. But he was silent and she said:
I cannot see which way you are pointing, the sky is so dark red,
And when the sandstorm is over I shall lie down on my bed.

TO A DEAD VOLE

Now Vole art dead
And done is all thy bleeding.
Thy soul is sped
And all thy body's heeding
For daily bread
And comfortable bed
Has brought thee where there's no more thought of feeding,
And where the soil is thy last unappreciated quilt.

REVERSIONARY

The Lion dishonoured bids death come,
The worm in like hap lingers on.
The Lion dead, his pride no less,
The world inherits wormliness.

DEAR KARL

Dear Karl, I send you Walt Whitman in a sixpenny book.
'How dilettante,' I hear you observe, 'I hate these selections
Arbitrarily made to meet a need that is not mine and a taste
Utterly antagonistic, wholly alien, egregiously coercionary

Of individualism's, egotism's, insolence's light-fingered
    traffickings.'
Put a leash on your indignation; hold it on a tight short leash,
Muzzle it in a tough criss-cross mesh of temporization and
    impartiality.
'God, I have no such dishonourable merchandise, such tinsel and
    tawdry in my shop window.'
So you say. Then borrow or steal a muzzle to muzzle your
    indignation,
A criss-cross wire mesh of temporization and suavity, and with a
    muzzled and leashed wrath
Hanging on your tapping heels: Listen.
If I had what hypocritical poetasters crocodilely whining call
    lucre and filthy,
But man, and it takes a man to articulate the unpalatable truth,
Means of support, if I had this and a little more,
I would give you Leaves of Grass, I would send
All of Walt Whitman to you with a smile that guesses it is
More blest to give than receive.
For I, I myself, I have no Leaves of Grass
But only Walt Whitman in a sixpenny book,
Taste's, blend's, essence's, multum-in-parvo's Walt Whitman.
And now sending it to you I say:
Fare out, Karl, on an afternoon's excursion, on a sixpenny
    unexplored uncharted road,
Over sixpennyworth of tarmac, blistered by an American sun,
    over irrupted boulders,
And a hundred freakish geology's superimpositions. Fare out on
    a strange road
Between lunchtime and dinner. Bon voyage, Karl, bon voyage.

IN CANAAN'S HAPPY LAND

Fair waved the golden corn
When I was stepping out,
And all the churchyard bells they rang
The day I turned about.

It's nice to get abroad,
It quickens and refines,
But now I find myself at home
My heart to peace inclines.

The bells ring for my friends
Who were untimely slain,
But I was luckier than they
And go my rounds again.

I take the cart I took,
I take another horse,
I sell my goods from door to door
And smother every curse.

PROUD DEATH WITH SWELLING PORT

Proud Death with swelling port comes ruffling by,
He takes the worthy man and leaves the fond.
So many worthy men and they must die,
And all the foolish men stay still beyond
The shadow of Death's beckoning. O let *them* go
And save man's nobler sons and daughters from Death's blow.

Thou wilt not do it, Lord, still wilt thou take
First fruits of our integrity and strength,
Tithes of our wisdom thou wilt have, and make
Our loftiest sons sink to a coffin's length.

O spare them Lord, take toll of lesser men,
For it is certain *they* will come again.

Men of great moral stature are not born
So easily as men of lesser worth.
But in the steep captivity forlorn
Of Time's entrail they slowly draw to birth.
After such long gestation, hast no ruth
To eat them up in the first flower of youth?

O spare our nobler sons and daughters, give
Them space to grow and feel their sinews' might
And hearts' full beat. O Father, let them live
Throughout life's day, and in the cool of Night
That is the cloak of natural death take them away.
But while the sun is up still let them stay.

MY SOUL

In the flame of the flickering fire
The sins of my soul are few
And the thoughts in my head are the thoughts of a bed
With a solitary view.
But the eye of eternal consciousness
Must blink as a bat blinks bright
Or ever the thoughts in my head be stilled
On the brink of eternal night.

Oh feed to the golden fish his egg
Where he floats in his captive bowl,
To the cat his kind from the womb born blind,
And to the Lord my soul.

Dear Female Heart, I am sorry for you,
You must suffer, that is all that you can do.
But if you like, in common with the rest of the human race,
You may also look most absurd with a miserable face.

HOW SLOWLY TIME LENGTHENS

How slowly time lengthens from a hated event.
In my youth I was humiliated in a guilty association –
Insinuator, flatterer, Board of Trade Surveyor, hypocrite,
Aha, Hildreth Parker, how have the years dealt with you?

THE RIVER HUMBER

No wonder
The river Humber
Lies in a silken slumber.

For it is dawn
And over the newly warm
Earth the mists turn,

Wrapping their gentle fringes
Upon the river where it hinges
Upon the perfect sleep of perfected images.

Quiet in the thought of its felicity,
A graven monument of sufficiency
Beautiful in every line the river sleeps complacently.

And hardly the dawn distinguishes
Where a miasma languishes
Upon the waters' farther reaches.

Lapped in the sleeping consciousness
Of its waves' happiness
Upon the mudbanks of its approaches,

The river Humber
Turns again to deeper slumber,
Deeper than deeps in joys without number.

Would he might come
Again and I
Upon his breast
Again might lie.

Would I had not
In foolish wrath
Driven him ever
From my path.

Would that the sun,
His day's course over,
Might that same day's
Lost dawn recover.

As vain as this
Vain prayer are all
Vain prayers that would
Past days recall.

Never shall sun
Now sunk away
Rise up again
On yesterday.

Never shall love
Untimely slain
Rise from the grave
And live again.

NOURISH ME ON AN EGG

Nourish me on an egg, Nanny,
And ply with bottled stout,
And I'll grow to be a man
Before the secret's out.

Nourish me on an egg, Nanny,
With bottled stout to drink,
And I'll grow to be a man
Before you can think.

Nourish me on an egg, Nanny,
Don't wring your hands and weep,
Bring me a glass of stout
And close my eyes in sleep.

SOUVENIR DE MONSIEUR POOP

I am the self-appointed guardian of English literature,
I believe tremendously in the significance of age:
I believe that a writer is wise at 50,
Ten years wiser at 60, at 70 a sage.
I believe that juniors are lively, to be encouraged with discretion
    and snubbed,
I believe also that they are bouncing, communistic, ill mannered
    and, of course, young.
But I never define what I mean by youth
Because the word undefined is more useful for general purposes
    of abuse.
I believe that literature is a school where only those who apply
    themselves diligently to their tasks acquire merit.

And only they after the passage of a good many years (see above).
But then I am an old fogey.
I always write more in sorrow than in anger.
I am, after all, devoted to Shakespeare, Milton,
And, coming to our own times,
Of course
Housman.
I have never been known to say a word against the established
classics,
I am in fact devoted to the established classics.
In the service of literature I believe absolutely in the principle of
division;
I divide into age groups and also into schools.
This is in keeping with my scholastic mind, and enables me to
trounce
Not only youth
(Which might be thought intellectually frivolous by pedants) but
also periodical tendencies,
To ventilate, in a word, my own political and moral philosophy.
(When I say that I am an old fogey, I am, of course, joking.)
English literature, as I see it, requires to be defended
By a person of integrity and essential good humour
Against the forces of fanaticism, idiosyncrasy and anarchy.
I perfectly apprehend the perilous nature of my convictions
And I am prepared to go to the stake
For Shakespeare, Milton,
And, coming to our own times,
Of course
Housman.
I cannot say more than that, can I?
And I do not deem it advisable, in the interests of the editor to
whom I am spatially contracted,
To say less.

UNSER VATER

(Originally entitled Vater Unser)
To the tune of the Londonderry Air.

Unser Vater,
Du Der im Himmel wohnst,
Behold thy child,
His prayers and his complaint.
He was conceived
In sin and born to set it on,
This sin is his,
His strength to act upon.
Oh, Father, heed
Thy child, let not the grave
Seal him in sin
Beyond thy power to save.
Strike at his strength,
Leave weakness only for her vaunt,
Unser Vater,
Du Der im Himmel wohnst.

GNÄDIGES FRÄULEIN

In the cold light of morning she was looking rather queer,
In the cold light of morning, with a ribbon round her hair,
And her youth lay behind her a long time for many a year.

For when she was young, they took her love away
And sent him to work, beyond the Mexique Bay,
And she thought of him and lost her wits and now her hair is gray

With an, Oh, if I think of him he'll come again to me,
And an, Oh, it was but a whim that took him o'er the sea;
And an, Oh, for all my eyes are dim they can look lovingly.

THE FRIEND

We needs must love the highest when we see it,
And having seen it knowing lower flee it.
But whither flee
Exiled from bliss
In these sad days
Of nothingness,
Shall we,
Trailing the tired wing of happier flights,
Hemmed in by lower presents mourn past heights,
And in a phrase
Of bitterness
Throw
All our woe?
No, gentle soul,
If fate and all the world have wronged thee,
And every spectre of despite has thronged thee,
Keep fast
Thy visionary past,
A part of present's whole
And but a part.
Thus happiness
And grief in thy stout heart
Shall range thee higher than th' angelic bands
Who know bliss but no smart
And serve
With happy but not midnight clenched hands

A lower place deserve.
But thou of present depth and former height
Has highest height attained and needst no flight.

THE LADS OF THE VILLAGE

The lads of the village, we read in the lay,
By medalled commanders are muddled away,
And the picture that the poet makes is not very gay.

Poet, let the red blood flow, it makes the pattern better,
And let the tears flow, too, and grief stand that is their begetter,
And let man have his self-forged chain and hug every fetter.

For without the juxtaposition of muddles, medals and clay,
Would the picture be so very much more gay,
Would it not be a frivolous dance upon a summer's day?

Oh sing no more: Away with the folly of commanders.
This will not make a better song upon the field of Flanders,
Or upon any field of experience where pain makes patterns the
    poet slanders.

THE PHOTOGRAPH

They photographed me young upon a tiger skin
And now I do not care at all for kith and kin,
For oh the tiger nature works within.

Parents of England, not in smug
Fashion fancy set on a rug
Of animal fur the darling you would hug,

For lately born is not too young
To scent the savage he sits upon,
And tiger-possessed abandon all things human.

'... AND THE CLOUDS RETURN
AFTER THE RAIN'

To the tune 'Worthy the Lamb'.

In a shower of tears I sped my fears
And lost my heavy pain,
But now my grief that knew relief
Is sultried o'er again.

Of leaf and flower of that first shower
No memories remain.
The clouds hang down in heavy frown
But still it does not rain.

Happy the man of simple span
Whose cry waits on his pain,
But there are some whose mouths are dumb
When the clouds return again.

OUT OF TIME

It is a formal and deserted garden
With many a flower bed and winding path.
A cupid stands and draws a bow at venture
Upon a marble bath.

All round his feet the eager ivy grows,
Stretches upon the stone, above the ground,
And in the ivy flowers the busy bee
Makes a melodious sound.

The air is languorous with summer scents
And still it lies upon the garden all
As still and secret as it stayed upon
A funeral.

The sun shines brightly in the upper air
And casts his beams upon the garden grass.
There spilled they lie a carpet of dull gold
Where shadows pass.

The garden gives to these primaeval beams
That strew its floor a plastered yellow tone
As of too mellow sunshine that brings on
A thunder stone.

It is an ominous enchanted garden
That can transmogrify the healthful rays,
Can hold and make them an essential part
Of unquiet days.

Ah me, the unquiet days they tread me down,
The hours and minutes beat upon my head.
I have spent here the time of three men's lives
And am not dead.

And even as I count the days that pass
I lose the total and begin again.
It is an evil garden out of Time
A place of pain.

THE CHILDREN OF THE CROSS

Oh cold and ferocious are the children of the cross,
They have captured us and bound us and their gain is our loss.
But straining to death
In the stench of the fire's breath
We leave lonely for ever the children of the cross.

FALLEN, FALLEN

The angel that rebellion raised
In moment of ecstatic rage
Is fallen, is fallen; his power is gauged.

Noted, by rote is had, the word is spoken.
Nothing remains but a falling star for a token,
A tale told by the fireside, a sword that is broken.

WILL EVER?

Will ever the stormy seas and the surges deep,
Swinging from left to right over the world,
Stay in their idiot pacing, silently sleep
In a memorial silence of precreation?

Alas for the crafty hand and the cunning brain
That took from silence and sleep the form of the world,
That bound eternity in a measuring chain
Of hours reduplicate and sequential days.

Would that the hours of time as a word unsaid
Turning had turned again to the hourless night,
Would that the seas lay heavy upon the dead,
The lightless dead in the grave of a world new drowned.

LITTLE BOY SICK

I am not God's little lamb
I am God's sick tiger.
And I prowl about at night
And what most I love I bite,
And upon the jungle grass I slink,
Snuff the aroma of my mental stink,
Taste the salt tang of tears upon the brink
Of my uncomfortable muzzle.
My tail my beautiful, my lovely tail,
Is warped.
My stripes are matted and my coat once sleek
Hangs rough and undistinguished on my bones.
O God I was so beautiful when I was well.
My heart, my lungs, my sinews and my reins
Consumed a solitary ecstasy,
And light and pride informed each artery.
Then I a temple, now a charnel house.
Then I a high hozannah, now a dirge.
Then I a recompense of God's endeavour,
Now a reproach and earnest of lost toil.
Consider, Lord, a tiger's melancholy
And heed a minished tiger's muted moan,
For thou art sleek and shining bright
And I am weary.
Thy countenance is full of light
And mine is dreary.

THE VIOLENT HAND

Angel most cynical
Cold and inimical,
With a smile of brass
On your cruel face

I think you will irritate me.
So much that you will make me
Risk at a touch
All that is at stake for me.
If I clutch
With violent hand the rosary
You dangle out of reach for me
I shall find out what it must be
Taken not given freely, injury.

HUMAN AFFECTION

Mother, I love you so.
Said the child, I love you more than I know.
She laid her head on her mother's arm,
And the love between them kept them warm.

A KING IN FUNERAL PROCESSION

He blinks he sighs
He is alive, they cry.

Give us the body
Let us see him breathe

Show us the heartbeat
And the dedicated sleeve.
He looks ill
They are satisfied he is looking that way
It is no more than he should
He looks ill
O.K.

De profundis
The solemn music the tune
Clamavi
I have cried unto thee on the loud bassoon
Clamavi a toto corde meo Domine
From the desert the stones
From the rift of this affectionate people
From my bones.

Lift the baby
Let her see him
Lift up the baby
Give her a lift up then

Oh Lord I am not high minded
I have no proud looks
Not one proud look they have left me
I am their picture book.

MURDER

Farewell for ever, well for ever fare,
The soul whose body lies beneath this stone!
Tis easy said by one who had a care
Soul should doff flesh. That has another tone?

My hand brought *Filmer Smith* to this strait bed –
Well, fare his soul well, fear not I the dead.

GIRLS!

Girls! although I am a woman
I always try to appear human

Unlike Miss So-and-So whose greatest pride
Is to remain always in the VI Form and not let down the side

Do not sell the pass dear, dont let down the side,
That is what this woman said and a lot of balsy stuff beside
(Oh the awful balsy nonsense that this woman cried.)

Girls! I will let down the side if I get a chance
And I will sell the pass for a couple of pence.

WHERE ARE YOU GOING?

Oh where are ye going ye human faces,
Where are ye going, to what far places,
Where are ye going, to what distances?

The boat takes the boatman,
The deep-sea fisher
Has taken away
The old world preacher,

This tedious old person who asked such questions
As drove everybody to exasperation.
No wonder they all of them cried, Good riddance!

AUTUMN

He told his life story to Mrs Courtly
Who was a widow. 'Let us get married shortly,'
He said. 'I am no longer passionate,
But we can have some conversation before it is too late.'

POET!

Poet, thou art dead and damned,
That speakst upon no moral text.
I bury one that babbled but; –
Thou art the next. Thou art the next.

THE ZOO

The lion sits within his cage,
Weeping tears of ruby rage,
He licks his snout, the tears fall down
And water dusty London town.

He does not like you, little boy,
It's no use making up to him,
He does not like you any more
Than he likes Nurse, or Baby Jim.

Nor would you do if you were he,
And he were you, for dont you see
God gave him lovely teeth and claws
So that he might eat little boys.

So that he might
In anger slay
The little lambs
That skip and play
Pounce down upon their placid dams
And make dams flesh to pad his hams.

So that he might
Appal the night
With crunching bones
And awful groans
Of antelope and buffalo,
And the unwary hunter whose 'Hallo'
Tells us his life is over here below.
There's none to help him, fear inspired,
Who shouts because his gun misfired.

All this the lion sees, and pants
Because he knows the hot sun slants
Between the rancid jungle-grass,
Which never more shall part to let him pass
Down to the jungle drinking-hole,
Whither the zebra comes with her sleek foal.

The sun is hot by day and has his swink,
And sops up sleepy lions' and tigers' stink,
But not this lion's stink, poor carnivore,
He's on the shady shelf for ever more.

His claws are blunt, his teeth fall out,
No victim's flesh consoles his snout,
And that is why his eyes are red
Considering his talents are misusèd.

ADVICE TO YOUNG CHILDREN

'Children who paddle where the ocean bed shelves steeply
Must take great care they do not,
Paddle too deeply.'

Thus spake the awful aging couple
Whose heart the years had turned to rubble.

But the little children, to save any bother,
Let it in at one ear and out at the other.

THE FACE

There is a face I know too well,
A face I dread to see,
So vain it is, so eloquent
Of all futility.

It is a human face that hides
A monkey soul within,
That bangs about, that beats a gong,
That makes a horrid din.

Sometimes the monkey soul will sprawl
Athwart the human eyes,
And peering forth, will flesh its pads,
And utter social lies.

So wretched is this face, so vain,
So empty and forlorn,
You well may say that better far
This face had not been born.

IF I LIE DOWN

If I lie down upon my bed I must be here,
But if I lie down in my grave I may be elsewhere.

CONVICTION (I)

Christ died for God and me
Upon the crucifixion tree
For God a spoken Word
For me a Sword
For God a hymn of praise
For me eternal days
For God an explanation
For me salvation.

CONVICTION (II)

I walked abroad in Easter Park,
I heard the wild dog's distant bark,
I knew my Lord was risen again, –
Wild dog, wild dog, you bark in vain.

CONVICTION (III)

The shadow was so black,
I thought it was a cat,
But once in to it
I knew it

No more black
Than a shadow's back.

Illusion is a freak
Of mind;
The cat's to seek.

CONVICTION (IV)

I like to get off with people,
I like to lie in their arms,
I like to be held and tightly kissed,
Safe from all alarms.

I like to laugh and be happy
With a beautiful beautiful kiss,
I tell you, in all the world
There is no bliss like this.

THE VIRTUOSO

The portrait of my mother,
In plaster lightly scored,
Has always protected me
From anything untoward;
In Manchester or Italy,
Wherever I have toured,
Upon its plinth
It beholds the zenith
Of my success on the pianoforte;
I ask no further reward,
I ask no further reward.

VILLAINS

Profit and Batten
Had coats lined with satin,
And no wonder either,
For they never owed a stiver;
If folks owed them rent,
They owed at ten per cent.
Sing Batten and Profit
If you've got a hat, doff it.

LE MAJEUR YDOW

'Eh bien! Marche!', fit le Majeur Ydow,
'Any more gentlemen like that? *I'll see them off!*'

But there were no gentlemen really, only the phantoms
He warred with in his perpetual tantrums.

THE LITTLE DAUGHTERS
OF AMERICA

Pearl Harbour, 1941.

Admirals Curse-You and No–More
Set their compasses and sailed for war.

I am sorry that all the little daughters of America
Should be involved in a thing like this; upon my word.

SHE SAID ...

She said as she tumbled the baby in:
There, little baby, go sink or swim,
I brought you into the world, what more should I do?
Do you expect me always to be responsible for you?

QUAND ON N'A PAS CE QUE L'ON
AIME, IL FAUT AIMER CE QUE L'ON A –

Cold as no love, and wild with all negation –
Oh Death in Life, the lack of animation.

THE CONVENTIONALIST

Fourteen-year-old, why must you giggle and dote,
Fourteen-year-old, why are you such a goat?
I'm fourteen years old, that is the reason,
I giggle and dote in season.

STUDY TO DESERVE DEATH

Study to deserve Death, they only may
Who fought well upon their earthly day,
Who never sheathed their swords or ran away.

See, such a man as this now proudly stands,
Pale in the clasp of Death, and to his hands
Yields up the sword, but keeps the laurel bands.

Honour and emulate his warrior soul,
For whom the sonorous death-bells toll;
He after journeying has reached his goal.

Prate not to me of suicide,
Faint heart in battle, not for pride
I say Endure, but that such end denied
Makes welcomer yet the death that's to be died.

DIRGE

From a friend's friend I taste friendship,
From a friend's friend love,
My spirit in confusion,
Long years I strove,
But now I know that never
Nearer I shall move,
Than a friend's friend to friendship,
To love than a friend's love.

Into the dark night
Resignedly I go,
I am not so afraid of the dark night

As the friends I do not know,
I do not fear the night above,
As I fear the friends below.

DISTRACTIONS AND THE
HUMAN CROWD

Ormerod was deeply troubled
When he read in philosophy and religion
Of man's lust after God,
And the knowledge of God,
And the experience of God
In the achievement of solitary communion and the loss of self.
For he said that he had known this knowledge,
And experienced this experience,
Before life and after death;
But that here in temporal life, and in temporal life only, was
    permitted,
(As in a flaw of divine government, a voluntary recession),
A place where man might impinge upon man,
And be subject to a thousand and one idiotic distractions.
And thus it was that he found himself
Ever at issue with the Schools,
For ever more and more he pursued the distractions,
Knowing them to be ephemeral, under time, peculiar,
And in eternity, without place or puff.
Then, ah then, he said, following the tea-parties,
(And the innumerable conferences for social rearrangement),
I knew, and shall know again, the name of God, closer than close;
But now I know a stranger thing,
That never can I study too closely, for never will it come again, –
Distractions and the human crowd.

BE OFF!

I'm sorry to say my dear wife is a dreamer,
And as she dreams she gets paler and leaner.
'Then be off to your Dream, with his fly-away hat,
I'll stay with the girls who are happy and fat.'

LOVE ME!

Love me, Love me, I cried to the rocks and the trees,
And Love me, they cried again, but it was only to tease.
Once I cried Love me to the people, but they fled like a dream,
And when I cried Love me to my friend, she began to scream.
Oh why do they leave me, the beautiful people, and only the rocks
    remain,
To cry Love me, as I cry Love me, and Love me again.

On the rock a baked sea-serpent lies,
And his eyelids close tightly over his violent eyes,
And I fear that his eyes will open and confound me with a
    mirthless word,
That the rocks will harp on for ever, and my Love me never be
    heard.

THE WILD DOG

The City Dog goes to the drinking trough,
He waves his tail and laughs, and goes when he has had enough.
His intelligence is on the brink
Of human intelligence. He knows the Council will give him a
    drink.

The Wild Dog is not such an animal,
Untouched by human kind, he is inimical,
He keeps his tail stiff, his eyes blink,
And he goes to the river when he wants a drink.
He goes to the river, he stamps on the mud,
And at night he sleeps in the dark wood.

LADY 'ROGUE' SINGLETON

Come, wed me, Lady Singleton,
And we will have a baby soon
And we will live in Edmonton
Where all the friendly people run.

I could never make you happy, darling,
Or give you the baby you want,
I would always very much rather, dear,
Live in a tent.

I am not a cold woman, Henry,
But I do not feel for you,
What I feel for the elephants and the miasmas
And the general view.

RENCONTRES FUNESTES

I fear the ladies and gentlemen under the trees,
Could any of them make an affectionate partner and not tease? –
Oh, the affectionate sensitive mind is not easy to please.

THE FILM STAR

Donnez à manger aux affamées
It is a film star who passes this way
He is looking so nice the women would like
To have him on a tray
Donnez à manger aux affamées.

THE BOTTLE OF ASPIRINS

'I look at the bottle, when mournful I feel.'
'C'est une ressource contre tout,' ajouta-t-il,
(Avec le sombre gaité du pays des suicides
D'où il était), – 'two hundred and I am freed,'
He said, 'from anxiety.'

THE GOVERNESS

The milky love of this bland child
Her governess has quite beguiled,
And now they spend the hours talking,
Sometimes winding wool and sometimes walking.

THE ACTRESS

I can't say I enjoyed it, but the pay was good.
Oh how I weep and toil in this world of wood!
Longing in the city for the pursuit of beautiful scenery,
I earn my bread upon the Stage, amid painted greenery.
I have a poet's mind, but a poor exterior,
What goes on inside me is superior.

THE DEVIL-MY-WIFE

To the tune of 'Golden slumbers'.

The nervous face of my dear wife
Is covered with a fearful grin,
And nods and becks
Come without checks
As the devils pop out and in.

Gush, then, gush and gabble,
Vanity is your dabble,
And in mediocrity
Is your cruelty.

THE REPENTANCE OF LADY T

I look in the glass
Whose face do I see?
It is the face
Of Lady T.

I wish to change,
How can that be?
Oh Lamb of God
Change me, change me.

THE SMILE

When ancient girl is garbed in spite
And turns to rend, and lives to bite,
Oh what can end the marriage night?

Wait, wait, (and with a smile); the dawn
Shall come again, and day return
As fair as any that has gone.

But if the nature of that smile
Be mockery, contempt and guile,
Should such a one my face defile?
No! rather let me *call* her – Crocodile!

FORGOT!

There is a fearful solitude
Within the careless multitude,
And in the open country too,

He mused, and then it seemed to him
The solitude lay all within;
He longed for some interior din:

Some echo from the worldly rout,
To indicate a common lot,
Some charge that he might be about,
But oh he felt that he was quite forgot.

A MAN I AM

I was consumed by so much hate
I did not feel that I could wait,
I could not wait for long at anyrate.
I ran into the forest wild,
I seized a little new born child,
I tore his throat, I licked my fang,
Just like a wolf. A wolf I am.

I ran wild for centuries
Beneath the immemorial trees,
Sometimes I thought my heart would freeze,
And never know a moment's ease.
But presently the spring broke in
Upon the pastures of my sin,
My poor heart bled like anything.
The drops fell down, I knew remorse,
I tasted that primordial curse,
And falling ill, I soon grew worse.
Until at last I cried on Him,
Before whom angel faces dim,
To take the burden of my sin
And break my head beneath his wing.

Upon the silt of death I swam
And as I wept my joy began
Just like a man. A man I am.

THE WHITE THOUGHT

I shall be glad to be silent, Mother, and hear you speak,
You encouraged me to tell too much, and my thoughts are weak,
I shall keep them to myself for a time, and when I am older
They will shine as a white worm shines under a green boulder.

IN THE NIGHT

I longed for companionship rather,
But my companions I always wished farther.
And now in the desolate night
I think only of the people I should like to bite.

THE MAGIC MORNING

The boating party
Started at dawn from Clarté.
Lightly lightly they stepped into the green boat
(The Lady Marion has left behind her golden coat).
Marion d'Arcy and Charley Dake
Were the only ones. He rowed her upon the lake.
He rowed her across the lake until the green shallows
Paled in a waxen lily litter striped with swallows.
And now the morning sun flecks the dark trees
And lightly the mauve sedge moves in a little breeze.

Charley Dake loves the ducal girl
But her eyelids flick flick upon his thoughts' whirl.
Oh my ducal girl, cries Charley in a fit
Of love-spasm. He is Cupid-hit.
But the Lady Marion smiles and smiles
And so they go again upon the watery miles.

'Oh Charley, Charley, do not go upon the water'
Cries a friendly swan, 'with the Duke's daughter.
You wish to marry er, my boy-carrier? you can not support er
Oh do not go with the Duke's daughter.'

There is an island in the lake, old brick walled,
Where the laurestina climbs and is not spoiled.
What man will spoil the brick walls of their yellow brim?
Such a one as is nervy bold and grim.
(Such a one, says the swan, as has something in store for him.)

Flick flick the eyelids of the lady mark
Where a dark angel flies across her father's park.
All the green grass shivers in a warning,
Flee, Charley, flee the magic morning.

But Charley is folly-blind to the visitation
Of the dark angel of consternation.
Boldly he plucks a golden cup
Throws it in Marion's lap and does not look up.

Ah then the thunder peals and the waters bound
For who took the flower, the angel says, must be drowned.
So up rears the lake water and drags him underneath
Where in suffering he draws his last breath.
'Never more', cries the swan, 'shall Charley be seen,
He is underneath the waters of the mis en scène.'
(And 'Charley, Charley, Charley' cry the swan-instructed
        curlews
Ever after as they fly to their nests in the purlieus.)

But the ducal girl comes safe to land and takes her coat,
And goes off in the likeness of a slim stoat.

APRÈS LA POLITIQUE, LA HAINE DES BOURBONS

Count Flanders
Was eaten up with pride;
His dog Sanders
Thought only of his inside.

They were a precious couple,
And let the people feed on straw and rubble.

Bitter was the weather,
Bitter the people,
When they flung Count Flanders
From the church steeple.
Bitter was the weather,
Iron the ground,
When Dog Sanders died of a stomach wound.

THE POETS ARE SILENT

There's no new spirit abroad,
As I looked, I saw;
And I say that it is to the poets' merit
To be silent about the war.

THE PLEASURES OF FRIENDSHIP

The pleasures of friendship are exquisite,
How pleasant to go to a friend on a visit!
I go to my friend, we walk on the grass,
And the hours and moments like minutes pass.

HAPPINESS

Happiness is silent, or speaks equivocally for friends,
Grief is explicit and her song never ends,
Happiness is like England, and will not state a case,
Grief like Guilt rushes in and talks apace.

LOT'S WIFE

*' In that rich, oil-bearing region, it is probable that Lot's wife was
turned into a pillar of asphalt – not salt.'*

Sir William Whitebait, Member of the Institute of Mining
Engineers

I long for the desolate valleys,
Where the rivers of asphalt flow,
For here in the streets of the living,
Where my footsteps run to and fro,
Though my smile be never so friendly,
I offend wherever I go.

Yes, here in the land of the living,
Though a marriage be fairly sprung,
And the heart be loving and giving,
In the end it is sure to go wrong.

Then take me to the valley of asphalt,
And turn me to a river of stone,
That no tree may shift to my sighing,
Or breezes convey my moan.

THE FOOL

A couple of women is one too many,
Oh, how I wish I could do without any!

NO MORE PEOPLE

Passing at my pleasure's pace
Among each moping angel face,
Above the sun on the lily-bright air
I fly my aeroplane here and there.
The heaven-born plod the heavens over,
But I, the son of mischief's lover,
Let the engine carry me. The angels, wing sore,
Look glum, I guess wish they were earth-born more and more.
But sometimes I have a feeling that my busy clatter
Has a mocking echo.
Than earth-born engine-borne, heaven-born wing-borne is
    better?
Do they look sideways because they know
That they will live to see the day when there are no more people?
All right. All right.
(I drop my bomb upon a church steeple.)

HAST DU DICH VERIRRT?

My child, my child, watch how he goes,
The man in Party coloured clothes.

SATIN-CLAD

Satin-clad, with many a pearl,
Is this rich and wretched girl.
Does she weep? Her tears are crystal,
And she counts them as they fall.

UNPOPULAR, LONELY AND LOVING

Unpopular, lonely and loving,
Elinor need not trouble,
For if she were not so loving,
She would not be so miserable.

'CECI EST DIGNE DE GENS SANS DIEU'

Allen

These hands so well articulated
By brother's life-blood are contaminated
And still he walks, and still the shadows fall,
He clasps them. There is nothing there at all.

WHEN THE SPARROW FLIES

When the sparrow flies to the delicate branch
He seems to be a heavy one alighting there,
It is March, and the fine twigs dance
As the boisterous sparrow plunges masterfully.

Fly again to my heart oh my beloved,
My heart flies too high when you are absent.

VOICES AGAINST ENGLAND IN THE NIGHT

'England, you had better go,
There is nothing else that you ought to do,
You lump of survival value, you are too slow.

England, you have been here too long,
And the songs you sing are the songs you sung
On a braver day. Now they are wrong.

And as you sing the sliver slips from your lips,
And the governing garment sits ridiculously on your hips.
It is a pity that you are still too cunning to make slips.'

Dr Goebbels, that is the point,
You are a few years too soon with your jaunt,
Time and the moment is not yet England's daunt.

Yes, dreaming Germany with your Urge and Night,
You must go down before English and American might.
It is well, it is well, cries the peace kite.

Perhaps England our darling will recover her lost thought,
We must think sensibly about our victory and not be distraught,
Perhaps America will have an idea, and perhaps not.

But they cried: Could not England, once the world's best,
Put off her governing garment and be better dressed
In a shroud, a shroud? O history turn thy pages fast!

'N'EST-CE PAS ASSEZ DE NE ME POINT HAÏR?'

Stand off, Mother, let me go!
The clock upon the shelf is slow
There wants but half a moment
E'er I am celled and barred in thy heart's convent.

Mother, if mother-love enclosure be,
It were enough, my dear, not quite to hate me.

THE FAILED SPIRIT

To those who are isolate
War comes, promising respite,
Making what seems to be up to the moment the most successful
    endeavour
Against the fort of the failed spirit that is alone for ever.
Spurious failed spirit, adamantine wasture,
Crop, spirit, crop thy stony pasture!

THE SLIDING MOUNTAIN

The terrors of the scenery,
The black rocks of the sliding mountain,
Are hid from the man of family
Who lives beneath the fountain.
His name is Domesticity,
He's married to an ivy tree,
And the little children laugh and scream,
For they do not know what these things mean.

THE RECLUSE

My soul within the shades of night,
Like a languid plant with a fungoid blight,
Shone out in unearthly damp a bright white light;
Pashy the ground underfoot where I trod,
Musing as I passed of the nature of God,
But on my reverent reveries and fruitful plod
Of tear-strewn steps, like a wrathful rod
Fell the touch of a girl, young in years and officious
Who broke at once at a touch my chain of delicious
Melancholy. Away flew every ecstasy.
With ridiculous intention she drew me to the sun,
My soul's rich languors decried,
And, e'er I could chide, away did run,
Leaving my soul undone.
O too much sun, O wretched presumption,
O too little wisdom and too much compunction.

'I COULD LET TOM GO – BUT WHAT ABOUT THE CHILDREN?'

Since what you want, not what you ought,
Is the difficult thing to decide,
I advise you, Amelia, to persevere
With Duty for your guide.

CHRISTMAS

A child is born, they cry, a child
And he is Noble and not Mild
(It is the child that makes them wild).

The King sits brooding on his throne
He looks around and calls a man:
My men bring me a heavy stone.

My men bring me a purple robe
And bring me whips and iron goad.
They brought them to him where he strode.

My men bring gold and bring incense
And fetch all noble children at once
That I shall never take offence.

The men fetched the noble children away
They lifted them up and cried: Hurray.
The King sat back and clapped their play.

All noble mild children are brought home
To the wicked King who has cast them down
And ground their bones on the heavy stone.

But the child that is Noble and not Mild
He lies in his cot. He is unbeguiled.
He is Noble, he is not Mild,
And he is born to make men wild.

TORQUEMADA

Uncle Torquemada,
does Beppo know about Jesus?

THE ROMAN ROAD

A Christian speaks to a Lion in the Arena.

Oh Lion in a peculiar guise,
Sharp Roman road to Paradise,
Come eat me up, I'll pay thy toll
With all my flesh, and keep my soul.

THE CASTLE

I married the Earl of Egremont,
I never saw him by day,
I had him in bed at night,
And cuddled him tight.

We had two boys, twins,
Tommy and Roly,
Roly was so fat
We called him Roly-poly.

Oh that was a romantic time,
The castle had such a lonely look,
The estate,
Heavy with cockle and spurge,
Lay desolate.

The ocean waves
Lapped in the castle caves.

Oh I love the ramshackle castle,
And the room
Where our sons were born.

Oh I love the wild
Parkland,
The mild
Sunshine.

Underneath the wall
Sleeps our pet toad,
There the hollyhocks grow tall.

My children never saw their father,
Do not know,
He sleeps in my arms each night
Till cockcrow.

Oh I love the ramshackle castle,
And the turret room
Where our sons were born.

TO DEAN INGE LECTURING ON ORIGEN

Listen, all of you, listen, all of you,
This way wisdom lies,
To reconcile with the simplicity of God
His contingent pluralities.

Oh, the wise man sat in his chair,
And oh, the people they would not hear,
They said, It is much too deep for us,
As they turned to the Differential Calculus.

Oh, if the people had only heard
Him,
Oh, if that wise man's word was not blurred,
Not dimmed.

BEHIND THE KNIGHT

Behind the Knight sits hooded Care,
And as he rides she speaks him fair,
She lays her hand in his sable muff,
Ride he never so fast he'll not cast her off.

HAROLD'S LEAP

Harold, are you asleep?
Harold, I remember your leap,
It may have killed you
But it was a brave thing to do.
Two promontories ran high into the sky,
He leapt from one rock to the other
And fell to the sea's smother.
Harold was always afraid to climb high,
But something urged him on,
He felt he should try.
I would not say that he was wrong,
Although he succeeded in doing nothing but die.
Would you?
Ever after that steep
Place was called Harold's Leap.
It was a brave thing to do.

A MOTHER'S HEARSE

The love of a mother for her child
Is not necessarily a beautiful thing
It can be compounded of pride and show
And exalt the self above every thing.

Oh why is that child so spoilt and horrible?
His mother has never neglected the trouble
Of giving him his will at every turn
And that is why his eyes do burn.

His eyes do burn with a hungry fire
His fingers clutch at the air and do not tire
He is a persecuting force
And as he grows older he grows worse.

And for his sake the friends are put down
And the happy people do not come round,
In pride and hostility against the world
This family upon itself is now curled.

Oh wretched they and wretched the friend
And this will continue without end
And all for a mother's love it was,
I say it were better a mother's hearse.

TOUCH AND GO

Man is coming out of the mountains
But his tail is caught in the pass.
Why does he not free himself
Is he not an ass?

Do not be impatient with him
He is bowed with passion and fret
He is not out of the mountains
He is not half out yet.

Look at his sorrowful eyes
His torn cheeks, his brow
He lies with his head in the dust
Is there no one to help him now?

No, there is no one to help him
Let him get on with it
Cry the ancient enemies of man
As they cough and spit.

The enemies of man are like trees
They stand with the sun in their branches
Is there no one to help my creature
Where he languishes?

Ah, the delicate creature
He lies with his head in the rubble
Pray that the moment pass
And the trouble.

Look he moves, that is more than a prayer,
But he is so slow
Will he come out of the mountains?
It is touch and go.

MAN IS A SPIRIT

Man is a spirit. This the poor flesh knows,
Yet serves him well for host when the wind blows,
Why should this guest go wrinkling up his nose?

THOUGHT IS SUPERIOR

Thought is superior to dress and circumstance,
It is thought pure thought that sets the world in a dance.
And what is the greatest thought since the world begun?
Galileo's discovery that the earth goes round the sun.

THE RIVER GOD

I may be smelly and I may be old,
Rough in my pebbles, reedy in my pools,
But where my fish float by I bless their swimming
And I like the people to bathe in me, especially women.
But I can drown the fools
Who bathe too close to the weir, contrary to rules.
And they take a long time drowning
As I throw them up now and then in a spirit of clowning.
Hi yih, yippity-yap, merrily I flow,
Oh I may be an old foul river but I have plenty of go.
Once there was a lady who was too bold
She bathed in me by the tall black cliff where the water runs cold,
So I brought her down here
To be my beautiful dear.
Oh will she stay with me will she stay
This beautiful lady, or will she go away?
She lies in my beautiful deep river bed with many a weed
To hold her, and many a waving reed.
Oh who would guess what a beautiful white face lies there
Waiting for me to smooth and wash away the fear
She looks at me with. Hi yih, do not let her
Go. There is no one on earth who does not forget her
Now. They say I am a foolish old smelly river
But they do not know of my wide original bed
Where the lady waits, with her golden sleepy head.
If she wishes to go I will not forgive her.

COOL AS A CUCUMBER

Cool as a cucumber calm as a mill pond sound as a bell
Was Mary
When she went to the Wishing Well.

But a fairy came up out of the well
And cursed her up hill and down dale
And cursed her from midnight to morning hail.

And now she gets worse and worse
Ever since she listened to the fairy's curse
She is nervy grim and bold
Looks over her left shoulder and does not do as she is told.

She is quite unfit for marriage
Of course
Since she listened to the fairy's curse
She grows worse and worse.

Starts off by herself each day
In a most unusual way
But nobody seems to know which way.

She looks pale, really unhealthy,
And moves so queerly, rather stealthy.

Mary come back to me,
Cried one who loved her.
He is the miller's son.
And when she heard him she broke into a run.

She has not been seen since then.
If you ask me she'll not be seen again.

THE ORPHAN REFORMED

The orphan is looking for parents
She roams the world over
Looking for parents and cover.
She looks at this pair and that
Cries, Father, Mother,
Likes these, does not like those,
Stays for a time; goes.
Crying, Oh hearts of stone.
But really she is better alone.
Orphan, the people who will not be your parents are not evil,
Not the devil.
But still she cries, Father, Mother
Must I be alone for ever?
Yes you must. Oh wicked orphan, oh rebellion,
Must an orphan not be alone is that your opinion?
At last the orphan is reformed. Now quite
Alone she goes; now she is right.
Now when she cries, Father, Mother, it is only to please.
Now the people do not mind, now they say she is a mild tease.

A SHOOTING INCIDENT

Man does not live by bread alone
Nor die alone for lack of it
For he may be well fed, and die,
Well housed, well married, still may die.
There is a hunger of the heart
Will slay him, though each day he feast
On bread and wine, and go well dresst,
And such a one was Colonel Yeast.

He was a noble simple man
But all within his heart was black
And as he walked the way along
He cried, alas alack,
And cried and sighed and sighed and cried,
I am a long-delayèd suicide.
It was as though a fiend had swung
Him by the toe when he was young
And swung him so
And to and fro
And swore and said he should be most oppressed
When most against a loving friend he pressed.
And now he walks with gun and roar –
He is a colonel in the Indian Army –
Sporting upon a tiger's spoor
And with him goes his faithful escort, Harmi.
Oh Harmi dear I love the sun
And all the crooked jungle path
But most the water holes I love
With creatures peering from above.
Why do I pick the wilder animal?
It is because he is not fanciful.
I had a dog in England once,
I loved him well, his name was Bunce,
And now I think I see him here,
And as I think, the scene grows clear,
An English scene. The colonel sighed.
The misty fells lay open wide
Upon his loving thought,
And dog Bunce ran again to start
The timid hare, and play his part
As he was taught.
Wild creatures' eyes, the colonel said,
Are innocent and fathomless,
And when I look at them I see

That they are not aware of me,
And oh I find and oh I bless
A comfort in this emptiness.
They only see me when they want
To pounce upon me in the hunt.
But in the tame variety
There couches an anxiety
As if they yearned, yet knew not what
They yearned for, nor they yearned for not.
And so my dog would look at me
And it was pitiful to see
Such love and such dependency.
The human heart is not at ease
With animals that look like these.
The colonel paused and wiped his brow,
He felt his words were too dramatic
But as he knew no English they
Were lost upon the Asiatic.
Ah me, the bitter bitter love,
Why must it be so bitter,
Or animal, or man, or tree –
Would not no love be better?
As still in recollection bound
The Colonel gazed upon the ground
It seemed his senses in a swound
Had left him quite,
Then turning to his gun again
And stamping on his heavy pain,
He loaded up and in the sight
Beheld a tiger stepping bright.
He steps so brightly to his death,
The colonel shot him through the teeth.
I had a dream I beat dear Bunce,
He said, with many a weal
Until he lay down at my feet

All red from toe to heel
Then in my dream I rose and fled,
Crying, The dog, the dog is dead.
Now, Harmi, mark, when daylight came,
My night and dream to shatter through
My dog came and so looked at me
I said, Why, Bunce, what's the matter with you?
Oh day and night, oh Holy Dove,
We slay the thing we most do love,
And it is pitiful to see
Our friends live but in memory.
But they are safe in memory
And are they not? the colonel said,
He turned and looked at Harmi so
That Harmi dropped his gun and fled.
When he came back again he found
The colonel dying of a wound,
And crying close upon the ground:
Oh bright bright blood that flows so bright
Within the wound myself did make
Oh jungle grass that drinks it up
And with my life thy thirst doth slake
Why has my hand this hour postponed
That sees me now with dust conjoined?
The Indian's tears fell like a blot
Upon the colonel's face
And carefully before he left
He put his hands in place.
Later upon his tomb, now grave now gay,
He daily danced to keep the fiends away.

'OH STUBBORN RACE OF CADMUS'
SEED ...'

It is the bird of burial
I invoke for my brother's funeral.
I throw the dust in Creon's eyes
Not my father is blind but my uncle is.
And when they have killed me I shall stand in the Dark Hall
And cry: Orcus, see that my sister does not suffer at all.

THE AMBASSADOR

Underneath the broad hat is the face of the Ambassador
He rides on a white horse through hell looking two ways.
Doors open before him and shut when he has passed.
He is master of the mysteries and in the market place
He is known. He stole the trident, the girdle,
The sword, the sceptre and many mechanical instruments.
Thieves honour him. In the underworld he rides carelessly.
Sometimes he rises into the air and flies silently.

PERSEPHONE

I am that Persephone
Who played with her darlings in Sicily
Against a background of social security.

Oh what a glorious time we had
Or had we not? They said it was sad
I had been good, grown bad.

Oh can you wonder can you wonder
I struck the doll-faced day asunder
Stretched out and plucked the flower of winter thunder?

Then crashed the sky and the earth smoked
Where are father and mother now? Ah, croaked
The door-set crone, Sun's cloaked.

Up came the black horses and the dark King
And the harsh sunshine was as if it had never been
In the halls of Hades they said I was queen.

My mother, my darling mother,
I loved you more than any other,
Ah mother, mother, your tears smother.

No not for my father who rules
The fair fields of Italy and sunny fools
Do I mourn where the earth cools.

But my mother, I loved and left her
And of a fair daughter bereft her,
Grief cleft her.

Oh do not fret me
Mother, let me
Stay, forget me.

But still she seeks sorrowfully,
Calling me bitterly
By name, Persephone.

I in my new land learning
Snow-drifts on the fingers burning,
Ice, hurricane, cry: No returning.

Does my husband the King know, does he guess
In this wintriness
Is my happiness?

DO TAKE MURIEL OUT

Do take Muriel out
She is looking so glum
Do take Muriel out
All her friends have gone.

And after too much pressure
Looking for them in the Palace
She goes home to too much leisure
And this is what her life is.

All her friends are gone
And she is alone
And she looks for them where they have never been
And her peace is flown.

Her friends went into the forest
And across the river
And the desert took their footprints
And they went with a believer.

Ah they are gone they were so beautiful
And she can not come to them
And she kneels in her room at night
Crying, Amen.

Do take Muriel out
Although your name is Death
She will not complain
When you dance her over the blasted heath.

THE WEAK MONK

The monk sat in his den,
He took the mighty pen
And wrote 'Of God and Men.'

One day the thought struck him
It was not according to Catholic doctrine;
His blood ran dim.

He wrote till he was ninety years old,
Then he shut the book with a clasp of gold
And buried it under the sheep fold.

He'd enjoyed it so much, he loved to plod,
And he thought he'd a right to expect that God
Would rescue his book alive from the sod.

Of course it rotted in the snow and rain;
No one will ever know now what he wrote of God and men.
For this the monk is to blame.

LE SINGE QUI SWING

To the tune of Green-sleeves.

Outside the house
The swinging ape
Swung to and fro,
Swung to and fro,
And when midnight shone so clear
He was still swinging there.

Oh ho the swinging ape,
The happy peaceful animal,
Oh ho the swinging ape,
I love to see him gambol.

THE BROKEN FRIENDSHIP

'My heart is fallen in despair'
Said Easter Ross to Jolie Bear.
Jolie answered never a word
But passed her plate as if she had not heard.

Mrs Ross is took to her bed
And kept her eye fixed on the bed-rail peg
'When I am dead roll me under the barrow,
And who but pretty Jolie shall carry the harrow.'

Jolie Bear is gone away
Easter Ross's heart is broke,
Everything went out of her
When Jolie never spoke.

THE AFTER-THOUGHT

Rapunzel Rapunzel let down your hair
It is I your beautiful lover who am here
And when I come up this time I will bring a rope ladder with me
And then we can both escape into the dark wood immediately.
This must be one of those things, as Edgar Allan Poe says
        somewhere in a book,
Just because it is perfectly obvious one is certain to overlook.

I wonder sometimes by the way if Poe isn't a bit introspective,
One can stand about getting rather reflective,
But thinking about the way the mind works, you know,
Makes one inactive, one simply doesn't know which way to go;
Like the centipede in the poem who was corrupted by the toad
And ever after never did anything but lie in the middle of the road,

Or the old gurus of India I've seen, believe it or not,
Standing seventy five years on their toes until they dropped.
Or Titurel, for that matter, in his odd doom
Crying : I rejoice because by the mercy of the Saviour I continue to
    live in the tomb.

What is that darling? You cannot hear me?
That's odd. I can hear you quite distinctly.

THE WANDERER

Twas the voice of the Wanderer, I heard her exclaim,
You have weaned me too soon, you must nurse me again,
She taps as she passes at each window pane,
Pray, does she not know that she taps in vain?

Her voice flies away on the midnight wind,
But would she be happier if she were within?
She is happier far where the night winds fall,
And there are no doors and no windows at all.

No man has seen her, this pitiful ghost,
And no woman either, but heard her at most,
Sighing and tapping and sighing again,
You have weaned me too soon, you must nurse me again.

NO CATEGORIES!

I cry I cry
To God who created me
Not to you Angels who frustrated me
Let me fly, let me die,
Let me come to Him.

Not to you Angels on the wing,
With your severe faces,
And your scholarly grimaces,
And your do this and that,
And your exasperating pit-pat
Of appropriate admonishment.

That is not what the Creator meant.
In the day of his gusty creation
He made this and that
And laughed to see them grow fat.

Plod on, you Angels say, do better aspire higher
And one day you may be like us, or those next below us,
Or nearer the lowest,
Or lowest,
Doing their best.

Oh no no, you Angels, I say,
No hierarchies I pray.

Oh God, laugh not too much aside
Say not, it is a small matter.
See what your Angels do; scatter
Their pride; laugh them away.

Oh no categories I pray.

THE DESERTER

The world is come upon me, I used to keep it a long way off,
But now I have been run over and I am in the hands of the hospital
    staff.
They say as a matter of fact I have not been run over it's
    imagination,
But they all admit I shall be kept in bed under observation.
I must say it's very comfortable here, nursie has such nice hands,
And every morning the doctor come and lances my tuberculous
    glands.
He says he does nothing of the sort, but I have my own feelings
    about that,
And what they are if you don't mind I shall keep under my hat.
My friend, if you call it a friend, has left me; he says I am a
    deserter to ill health,
And that the things I should think about have made off for ever,
    and so has my wealth.
Portentous ass, what to do about him's no strain
I shall quite simply never speak to the fellow again.

I RODE WITH MY DARLING ...

I rode with my darling in the dark wood at night
And suddenly there was an angel burning bright
Come with me or go far away he said
But do not stay alone in the dark wood at night.

My darling grew pale he was responsible
He said we should go back it was reasonable
But I wished to stay with the angel in the dark wood at night.

My darling said goodbye and rode off angrily
And suddenly I rode after him and came to a cornfield
Where had my darling gone and where was the angel now?
The wind bent the corn and drew it along the ground
And the corn said, Do not go alone in the dark wood.

Then the wind drew more strongly and the black clouds covered
    the moon
And I rode into the dark wood at night.

There was a light burning in the trees but it was not the angel
And in the pale light stood a tall tower without windows
And a mean rain fell and the voice of the tower spoke,
Do not stay alone in the dark wood at night.

The walls of the pale tower were heavy, in a heavy mood
The great stones stood as if resisting without belief.
Oh how sad sighed the wind, how disconsolately,
Do not ride alone in the dark wood at night.

Loved I once my darling? I love him not now.
Had I a mother beloved? She lies far away.
A sister, a loving heart? My aunt a noble lady?
All all is silent in the dark wood at night.

GOD AND MAN

Man is my darling, my love and my pain,
My pleasure, my excitement, and my love again,
My wisdom, my courage, my power, my all,
Oh Man, do not come to me until I call.

In man is my life, and in man is my death,
He is my hazard, my pride and my breath,
I sought him, I wrought him, I pant on his worth,
In him I experience indeterminate growth.

Oh Man, Man, of all my animals dearest,
Do not come till I call, though thou weariest first.

MR OVER

Mr Over is dead
He died fighting and true
And on his tombstone they wrote
Over to You.

And who pray is this You
To whom Mr Over is gone?
Oh if we only knew that
We should not do wrong.

But who is this beautiful You
We all of us long for so much
Is he not our friend and our brother
Our father and such?

Yes he is this and much more
This is but a portion
A sea-drop in a bucket
Taken from the ocean

So the voices spake
Softly above my head
And a voice in my heart cried: Follow
Where he has led

And a devil's voice cried: Happy
Happy the dead.

MY CATS

I like to toss him up and down
A heavy cat weighs half a Crown
With a hey do diddle my cat Brown.

I like to pinch him on the sly
When nobody is passing by
With a hey do diddle my cat Fry.

I like to ruffle up his pride
And watch him skip and turn aside
With a hey do diddle my cat Hyde.

Hey Brown and Fry and Hyde my cats
That sit on tombstone for your mats.

DRUGS MADE PAULINE VAGUE

Drugs made Pauline vague.
She sat one day at the breakfast table
Fingering in a baffled way
The fronds of the maidenhair plant.

Was it the salt you were looking for dear?
Said Dulcie, exchanging a glance with the Brigadier.

Chuff chuff Pauline what's the matter?
Said the Brigadier to his wife
Who did not even notice
What a handsome couple they made.

OUR BOG IS DOOD

Our Bog is dood, our Bog is dood,
They lisped in accents mild,
But when I asked them to explain
They grew a little wild.
How do you know your Bog is dood
My darling little child?

We know because we wish it so
That is enough, they cried,
And straight within each infant eye
Stood up the flame of pride,
And if you do not think it so
You shall be crucified.

Then tell me, darling little ones,
What's dood, suppose Bog is?
Just what we think, the answer came,
Just what we think it is.
They bowed their heads. Our Bog is ours
And we are wholly his.

But when they raised them up again
They had forgotten me

Each one upon each other glared
In pride and misery
For what was dood, and what their Bog
They never could agree.

Oh sweet it was to leave them then,
And sweeter not to see,
And sweetest of all to walk alone
Beside the encroaching sea,
The sea that soon should drown them all,
That never yet drowned me.

WRETCHED WOMAN

Wretched woman that thou art
How thou piercest to my heart
With thy misery and graft
And thy lack of household craft.

LIGHTLY BOUND

You beastly child, I wish you had miscarried,
You beastly husband, I wish I had never married.
You hear the north wind riding fast past the window? He calls me.
Do you suppose I shall stay when I can go so easily?

LE REVENANT

My Uncle from the realms of Death
Returned to draw an earthly breath
And as he walked upon the heath
The wild wind whistled through his teeth.

He came unto a habitation
That was the centre of the nation
He knocked upon each house and said:
It is much better to be dead.

And when they stoned him from the door
He vowed he would come back no more.

TO SCHOOL!

Let all the little poets be gathered together in classes
And let prizes be given to them by the Prize Asses
And let them be sure to call all the little poets young
And worse follow what's bad begun
But do not expect the Muse to attend this school
Why look already how far off she has flown, she is no fool.

TO AN AMERICAN PUBLISHER

You say I must write *another* book? But I've just written this one.
You liked it so much that's the reason? Read it again then.

THE REHEARSAL

I always admire a beautiful woman
And I've brought you some flowers for your beautiful bosom.

DEATH-BED OF A FINANCIER

Deal not with me God as I have dealt with Man
In the prosperity which thou hast given me
Helpless in his need a careless course I ran
And now oh Lord that thou hast driven me
To my last gasp, I pray for all I am not worth
Deal not with me as I have dealt on earth.

THE HAT

I love my beautiful hat more than anything
And through my beautiful hat I see a wedding ring
The King will marry me and make me his own before all
And when I am married I shall wear my hat and walk on the
    palace wall.

THE RIDE

Riding slowly along the banks of a canal
Where the dredges had been at work and the slime lay piled,
I rode in Egypt slowly, slowly with Captain Fairchild,
Under a black sun, on an oppressive afternoon.
Pricking our dull horses to an even pace
We rode beside the black slime, mile upon mile,
Between the slime mounds, beside the black deep water.
Suddenly the captain turning smiled into my face,
Smiling with a black smile, pale beneath his burnt skin,
Smiling he said, If the Sultana of Istanbuol
Had in her Household a Grand Vizier so old
That he was alive in the Napoleonic Wars,
What is it, he said, she would most wish him to forget?
My hand for a moment lay slack upon the rein,
And my horse checking stood still with lowered head,
Oh, I said carelessly, the slime and the black slime,
The slime and the length and the slime
Of the ramshackle Ottoman Empire.
Well my dear chap, said the Captain smiling,
It always comes to that, but we know do we not,
That the slime and the black slime is something we can parry
With a Byronic connotation and a note in time.

I AM

Far from normal far from normal far from normal I am
He sighed as he stood on the river bank and watched where the
    fishes swam
But ever the wind in the willow trees whispered, I am; I am.
He saw the variety of nature

The ant the mole and the sky
And resignedly hurried upon his way
Crying: I, I; I, I;

Then a priest came and told him if he was good
And thought as he ought and did as he should
He should be saved by the Lamb's fresh blood.

Oh I know, I know the poor man cries,
I know the worth of the heavenly prize
And I know the strength of the race to be run
But my black heart cleaves to the strength of my gun.

Then he put his gun to his head and shot
Crying absurdly, I am not.

THE CROWN OF BAYS

They gave him a crown of bays and dressed him up,
But he was listless though famous, he had had enough.
He looked at the audience, they are clapping knaves,
And turning to the Winged Form, Who are you? he says.
'I am the Angel of the Considered Bays.'
When you go back I will follow you, he said.
'To do that, you must be dead.'
I ask it; this people is a basket.

He laid his head in the angel's lap,
Oh let me come with you, let me come.
'Can you say farewell to the people in deep slumbers
Who travel by the Underground railway with happy faces in
    numbers?'
These, and these
He said (thinking of the sleepers and the audience) tease,

Let me come with you.
'Only those who expect everything are prepared to take nothing,'
Said the angel slyly, as posing a conundrum,
'Death may be that.'
Still lead; I follow, pat pat.
'Can you say farewell to the Natural Beauties?'
Yes, I look at them through a glass cage, the glaze sullies.

The angel waved a hand and under a tree,
A mighty chestnut whose fine branches
The spring with white flowers enhances,
Lay the bay-crowned Misery.

Oh Angel of Bays, he cries, weeping bitterly,
You have forged a dagger with your visions for my penalty,
Crack my heart, pierce throat, I will come with you,
I only used to think it was worth while living for the view.
How beautiful the sky is that is bright blue
Through the green leaves, and the sun warms through and
        through
Before a man hangs they give him what he likes to eat,
So you have given me what I like to see, the trees and no street,
Now to the scaffold, Angel, do your part,
I will come with you. (The angel stabs him to the heart.)

As he lay bleeding his last into the untrod earth
He smiled a happy smile and said:
I had a philosophy of use and wont, it was bad;
I conceded that life was a balance with
Only three ha'pence to the liver's credit.
But to live with three ha'pence was a merit.
I held that nothing to have not wholly bad not wholly good
Was a young man's dream and juvenile aspiration,
Now I am come to that young man's situation,
And expecting everything gladly receive annihilation.

'You receive what I do not know,'
Said the angel, and with this word
Flies away and leaves him lying upon the sward.
But over his shoulder airborne came these last words, 'Briefly
In my opinion for what it is worth, you die trivially.'

A JEW IS ANGRY WITH HIS
FRIEND WHO DOES NOT
BELIEVE IN CIRCUMCISION

Oh ho uncircumciséd Sadducee I see
In all created time not one as thee
Befoul the cradle whence he came
Take a great name and make it a great shame
Take it and make it on the lips of the heathen a gibe
Not the name of a sect, not Sadducee, Pharisee or Scribe
But Jew Jew Jew
Should have taught you all that we knew
With a racial knowledge in the Pentateuchal days of old
Before the time had come for Sadducees to be so very bold
As to be so bold as to be too modern for circumcision
Oh mockery of Greek and Roman, oh derision
Of the derided
Now I have you, mannikin, depend
I'll dock you of your foreskin and something else that will end
All hope of posterity, no little Sadducees will you beget
When I've finished with you, but sit in a eunochy fret
Waiting for death to relieve you of a hated life
You look a little pale? What ho, a knife, a knife.

FROM THE COPTIC

Three angels came to the red red clay
Where in a heap it formless lay,

Stand up, stand up, thou lazy red clay,
Stand up and be Man this happy day.

Oh in its bones the red clay groaned,
And why should I do such a thing? it said,
And take such a thing on my downy head?
Then the first angel stood forth and said,

Thou shalt have happiness, thou shalt have pain,
And each shall fall turn and about again,
And no man shall say when the day shall fall
That thou shalt be happy or not at all.

And the second angel said much the same
While the red clay lay flat in the falling rain,
Crying, I will stay clay and take no blame.

Then the third angel rose up and said,
Listen thou clay, raise thy downy head,
When thou hast heard what I have to say
Thou shalt rise Man and go man's way.

What have you to promise? the red clay moans,
What have you in store for my future bones?
I am Death, said the angel, and death is the end,
I am Man, cries clay rising, and you are my friend.

A HUMANE MATERIALIST AT
THE BURNING OF A HERETIC

When shall that fuel fed fire grown fatter
Burn to consumption and a pitter patter
Of soft ash falling in a formless scatter
Telling Mind's death in a dump of Matter.

IN PROTOCREATION

In protocreation
Is my imagination
And in the world's first emergence from gaseous fire
My desire.
Then heaved the earth
In a first vegetable birth
Later according to the record
Experimental animals walked abroad.
The awkward pterodactyl
The brontosaurus
The mammoth and the early lizard
Were before us.
Oh had it but stopped then
Oh had there not come men.
Earth fired
And the seas smoked
Heavy heavy swung the swamp
Crust broke and the mountains poked.
Oh had it but stopped then
Oh had there not come men.
In that high and early time
There was no good deed and no crime
No oppression by informed mind
No knowledge and no human kind.

DO NOT!

Do not despair of man, and do not scold him,
Who are you that you should so lightly hold him?
Are you not also a man, and in your heart
Are there not warlike thoughts and fear and smart?
Are you not also afraid and in fear cruel,
Do you not think of yourself as usual,
Faint for ambition, desire to be loved,
Prick at a virtuous thought by beauty moved?
You love your wife, you hold your children dear,
Then say not that Man is vile, but say they are.
But they are not. So is your judgement shown
Presumptuous, false, quite vain, merely your own
Sadness for failed ambition set outside,
Made a philosophy of, prinked, beautified
In noble dress and into the world sent out
To run with the ill it most pretends to rout.
Oh know your own heart, that heart's not wholly evil,
And from the particular judge the general,
If judge you must, but with compassion see life,
Or else, of yourself despairing, flee strife.

THE DEATH SENTENCE

Cold as No Plea,
Yet wild with all negation,
Weeping I come
To my heart's destination,
To my last bed
Between th' unhallowed boards –
The Law allows it
And the Court awards.

THE COMMUTED SENTENCE

Shut me not alive away
From the light of every day
Hang me rather by the neck to die
Against a morning sky.

Oh shut me not behind a prison wall
I have a horror of this sort of place
Where I may sit and count the hours pass
And never see a smiling human face.

Here is all straight and narrow as a tomb
Oh shut me not within a little room.

Kathleen ni Houlihan
Walking down the boule-igan
Ran into a hooligan
Ah ha, Kathleen ni Houlihan.

She went with the rat-ican
And very soon they had a brat-ican
Ah ha, Kathleen ni Houlihan
How goes it now?

They called him Rebel-can
Oh he was a devil-can
Kathleen ni Houlihan
Your son.

And the big black cat-ican
That sat on the mat-ican
With a pit and a pati-can
Spit. Spat.

Was the chief sport
Of the Houlihan sort
And chiefly did Rebel-can
Twitch his tail, the devil-can.

All up the boule-igan
Runs Kathleen ni Houlihan
For flirting his tail the cat is gone,
They are alone.

And that is how the Houlihan
Fell out in the boule-igan
Whose tail shall they twitch now?
Eh, Kathleen, the cat is gone.

THE LEADER

Men fear the hollow man at the top of the tree
He is supported they say by a phoney majority
But the squirrel brings nuts and the mole brings meal
And the cock brings the spur from the tip of his heel
And they none of them dare say what they feel
For he kills as he wills does that horrible He
Who sits at the top of the old oak tree.

Oh foolish they are who keep his rules
And bring him food, they are surely fools
When it is plain as a pikestaff bold
They should run him out in the cold, cold, cold
Or burn him up in the hot fury
Of a flame that will lick to the top of a tree.

Oh if they only had some sense
The squirrel might store for her own expense
The cock at his heel find a use for the spur
And the mole with the meal sleek the young mole's fur.

But they will not do it, they are so frightened
Of what they have raised and the tree has heightened
Then come along come with a sigh and a leap
For this people runs mad in the Fuehrer Prinzip.

Yes they will have a lord and it matters not who
Be he hollow as a drum he will do, do, do.

OH, IF ONLY . . .

The intellectual Englishman shrank away from the bedside.
There in the bed lay the Englishwoman Blah in the arms of Captain
    Thomas.
Oh, the ineffable smug look of Blah (thought the young
    intellectual)
The satisfaction, the noble-animal dignity, the imperial
    carelessness!
As Blah lay smiling in her sleep, a shadow crossed the face of
    Thomas.
He awoke, and putting his arm across Blah's breast
He stared in a sullen and offended manner at the young intellectual.
Go to hell, cried Thomas. Go to hell, cried the young intellectual.
A purely nervous situation for you I fancy, sneered Thomas.
The young intellectual crept weeping away,
Oh, if he could only experience emotional extravagance!

WHO SHOT EUGENIE?

    We had ridden three days Eugenie and I
    And kept hidden
    By an unnecessary habitual caution
    The papers of our commission.

    How blank is the heart when on service bent
    Empty of all but official content
    So inappropriate is all individual consideration
    So impossible in the individual a communal realization
    Of states', peoples', any group-mind's preoccupation,
    That a girl in the service of her country at war
    Must have a mind as blank as a wall

Apt only to carry
The terms of her commission and hurry.

Eugenie and I in an open deserted country
Had travelled till nightfall of the third day
When putting our horses at a hedge at the top of a hill,
Up and over,
We found ourselves under cover
Of a mighty forest whose pines' green needles
Fallen carpeted the ground and silenced our horses' footfall.

Now night was entrenched and over our head the stars
Shone out their fitful rather disturbing light
That hardly served to penetrate the gloomy thread
Of the long forest ride we rode upon.

Why is it starlight so disturbs our kind
Dissipates the purposes of the human mind
Emptying familiar things of all significance
Setting the thoughts in an inconsequent dance
And making the loftiest and ruling of them sit mumchance?
I said no word of this to her nor she to me,
We were old campaigners both of us you see,
Only we rode, she as I, distracted
And the heart had gone out of us both and the virtue,
We rode in silence.

Hour by hour of the night we rode and the sickle moon
Clearing the feathered treetops soared overhead
And the path we followed led always towards the north,
Skirting a lake. We saw where the arms of trees
Old wood and rotten and allowed to rot and to fall
When it should have been chopped and cherished in the service of
    nations

(According to the best interpretation of King's Regulations)
Broke surface.
Over our shoulders from the right the moonlight shimmered
Down and across the waters of the forest lake
Making in semblance more sombre the shadowy margin.
We were glad to leave it, the sombre sinister pool,
And rode till daylight came and the cold dawn wind,
And the stars grew pale, and the moon sank down on the west.

In the gray of the early day we dismounted and watered our beasts,
And breakfasted there by the side of the cold clear spring,
And tethered our horses, and lay and rested and slept,
The sleep of exhaustion. And still no sound,
No least hurry or flurry of wild birds moving,
Spoke of the alien presence of human beings,
The forest enclosed us around and my dreams were always
Of ways without ending and passively hostile Nature,
Of forests deploying and advancing with the power of death
In the huddle of trees and the treacherous undergrowth.

The sun was hot on my face when I woke, and Eugenie was dead,
Shot, with a bullet through her head.
Yet every chamber in her revolver was full to plenty
And only in my own is there one that is empty.

FULL WELL I KNOW

Full well I know the flinty heart
That beats beneath those gentle airs
That asks the people to her hearth
But for a writer's cares
That asks them from below above
But only to observe, not love.

Then also as a writer she must fail
Since art without compassion don't avail?

VOICES ABOUT THE
PRINCESS ANEMONE

Underneath the tangled tree
Lies the pale Anemone.

She was the first who ever wrote
The word of fear, and tied it round her throat.

She ran into the forest wild
And there she lay and never smiled.

Sighing, Oh my word of fear
You shall be my only dear.

They said she was a princess lost
To an inheritance beyond all cost.

She feared too much they said, but she says, No,
My wealth is a golden reflection in the stream below.

She bends her head, her hands dip in the water
Fear is a band of gold on the King's daughter.

DEEPLY MORBID

Deeply morbid deeply morbid was the girl who typed the letters
Always out of office hours running with her social betters
But when daylight and the darkness of the office closed about her

Not for this ah not for this her office colleagues came to doubt her
It was that look within her eye
Why did it always seem to say goodbye?

Joan her name was and at lunchtime
Solitary solitary
She would go and watch the pictures
In the National Gallery
All alone all alone
This time with no friend beside her
She would go and watch the pictures
All alone.

Will she leave her office colleagues
Will she leave her evening pleasures
Toil within a friendly bureau
Running later in her leisure?
All alone all alone
Before the pictures she seems turned to stone.

Close upon the Turner pictures
Closer than a thought may go
Hangs her eye and all the colours
Leap into a special glow
All for her, all alone
All for her, all for Joan.

First the canvas where the ocean
Like a mighty animal
With a really wicked motion
Leaps for sailors' funeral

Holds her panting. Oh the creature
Oh the wicked virile thing
With its skin of fleck and shadow

Stretching tightening over him.
Wild yet captured wild yet captured
By the painter, Joan is quite enraptured.

Now she edges from the canvas
To another loved more dearly
Where the awful light of purest
Sunshine falls across the spray,
There the burning coasts of fancy
Open to her pleasure lay.
All alone, all alone
Come away, come away
All alone.

Lady Mary. Lady Kitty
The Honourable Featherstonehaugh
Polly Tommy from the office
Which of these shall hold her now?
Come away, come away
All alone.

The spray reached out and sucked her in
It was a hardly noticed thing
That Joan was there and is not now
(Oh go and tell young Featherstonehaugh)
Gone away, gone away
All alone.

She stood up straight
The sun fell down
There was no more of London Town
She went upon the painted shore
And there she walks for ever more

Happy quite
Beaming bright
In a happy happy light
All alone.

They say she was a morbid girl, no doubt of it
And what befell her clearly grew out of it
But I say she's a lucky one
To walk for ever in that sun
And as I bless sweet Turner's name
I wish that I could do the same.

THE GHOST OF WARE

I look in the mirror,
Whose face is there?
It is the face
Of the Ghost of Ware.
This is an old house,
The river flows below placidly,
I am enchanted completely
By this ancient city.
I will never leave you,
Dear town of Ware,
I will look into the mirror
Another afternoon and there
I shall see the smiling face
Of the Ghost of Ware.

NOT WAVING BUT DROWNING

Nobody heard him, the dead man,
But still he lay moaning:
I was much further out than you thought
And not waving but drowning.

Poor chap, he always loved larking
And now he's dead
It must have been too cold for him his heart gave way,
They said.

Oh, no no no, it was too cold always
(Still the dead one lay moaning)
I was much too far out all my life
And not waving but drowning.

In the graveyard, in the graveyard
By the tomb of Alan Blair
On the mighty Scottish mountain
Knelt the English visitor.

Oh my darling why did you leave me
To lie so cold where I cannot come,
I only wished to have you by me
In the busy town.

How beautiful are the Scottish mountains
Their backs are like ancient mammoths so quiet
And I should like to walk on the mountain
While it is light.

The people frowned to see her looking,
Alas for Alan that fell in with such a woman
Why is she here, what has brought her?
She has no thought for him.

The Englishwoman rose up quickly
And ran through the gates of the cemetery
And leapt on the mountain boulders
With quick step lightly,
Is that an eagle in the sky wheeling?
No, it is not wheeling but weaving
And it's too small for an eagle, it is not hard
To tell it is a buzzard.

Oh why are the people so hostile, why are they angry?
They say I come too late
And that Alan's blood is upon me
But chiefly it is my walking they hate.

Then the beautiful woman ran up the mountainside
As over the top she was spinning
And the people said she would never think of Alan again
And it was typical of Englishwomen.
But No, said an angel, you are wrong
She will think of him freely and frequently
She is not less sorry than you are
Only she was brought up differently.

'WHAT IS SHE WRITING?
PERHAPS IT WILL BE GOOD'

What is she writing? Perhaps it will be good,
The young girl laughs: 'I am in love.'
But the older girl is serious: 'Not now, perhaps later.'
Still the young girl teases: 'What's the matter?
To lose everything! A waste of time!'
But now the older one is quite silent,
Writing, writing, and perhaps it will be good.
Really neither girl is a fool.

THE FAIRY BELL

*A renegade poet, having taken to journalism for more money, is
rebuked by his Muse in the form of an old gentleman; he cuts her
throat.*

A dismal bell hung in the belfry
And clanged a dismal tune
And back and forth the bats did fly
Wherever there was room.

He seemed a melancholy but a reasonable creature,
Yet I could see about his hat as it were this belfry steeple.

The agony through which I go,
He said, is something that you ought to know
And something that you will know too
When I have finished telling you.

He took my hand, I could not choose but stand,
Perhaps for his own sake he should not have done this?
Yet I thought Death was the best prize, if he won this.

Oh, the sad music of the backward and forth
Flying of the bats, pleading for worth,
But in this perhaps again I was wrong –
That there was for him some enchantment in their song?

It is done now and I cannot trouble to rue it,
I took his gullet in my hand and with my knife cut through it.

But still in my head I sometimes hear the soft tune
Of the belfry bats moaning to find more room
And the ding-dong of that imaginary sound
Is as grateful as a fairy bell tolling by waters drowned.

THE NEW AGE

Shall I tell you the signs of a New Age coming?
It is a sound of drubbing and sobbing
Of people crying, We are old, we are old
And the sun is going down and becoming cold
Oh sinful and sad and the last of our kind
If we turn to God now do you think He will mind?

Then they fall on their knees and begin to whine
That the state of Art itself presages decline
As if Art has anything or ever had
To do with civilization whether good or bad.
Art is wild as a cat and quite separate from civilization
But that is another matter that is not now under consideration.
Oh these people are fools with their sighing and sinning
Why should Man be at an end? he is hardly beginning.
This New Age will slip in under cover of their cries
And be upon them before they have opened their eyes.
Well, say geological time is a one-foot rule
Then Man's only been here about half an inch to play the fool
Or be wise if he likes, as he often has been
Oh heavens how these crying people spoil the beautiful geological
  scene.

THE BLUE FROM HEAVEN

A legend of King Arthur of Britain.

King Arthur rode in another world
And his twelve knights rode behind him
And Guinevere was there
Crying: Arthur, where are you dear?

Why is the King so blue
Why is he this blue colour?
It is because the sun is shining
And he rides under the blue cornflowers.

High wave the cornflowers
That shed the pale blue light
And under the tall cornflowers
Rides King Arthur and his twelve knights.

And Guinevere is there
Crying: Arthur, where are you dear?

First there were twelve knights riding
And then there was only one
And King Arthur said to the one knight,
Be gone.

All I wish for now, said Arthur,
Is the beautiful colour blue
And to ride in the blue sunshine
And Guinevere I do not wish for you.

Oh Lord, said Guinevere
I do not see the colour blue
And I wish to ride where our knights rode,
After you.

Go back, go back, Guinevere,
Go back to the palace, said the King.
So she went back to the palace
And her grief did not seem to her a small thing.

The Queen has returned to the palace
Crying: Arthur, where are you dear?
And every day she speaks of Arthur's grandeur
To the knights who are there.

That Arthur has fallen from the grandeur
Of his powers all agree
And the falling off of Arthur
Becomes their theme presently.

As if it were only temporarily
And it was not for ever
They speak, but the Queen knows
He will come back never.

Yes, Arthur has passed away
Gladly he has laid down his reigning powers
He has gone to ride in the blue light
Of the peculiar towering cornflowers.

THE LADY OF THE WELL-SPRING

Renoir's 'La Source'.

He is quite captive to the Lady of the Well-Spring,
Who will rescue him?
Into the French drawing-room the afternoon sun shone
And as the French ladies laughed their white faces
Barred by the balcony shadows seemed to make grimaces.
In a far corner of the room
Sat the English child Joan
As far away as she could get but without exasperation
Only to be freed from the difficulty of conversation.
'Quite captive to the lady of the Well-Spring
Who will rescue him?'
Now I have an excuse to go
Said Joan, and walked out of the window
Down the iron staircase and along the path
And then she began to run through the tall wet grass.
Overhead the hot sun slanting
Fell on Joan as she ran through the fields panting,
Faster faster uphill she goes hoping
That as the ground goes uphill steeply sloping

She will find the well-spring. Into a little wood
She runs, the branches catching at her feet draw blood
And there is a sound of piping screaming croaking clacking
As the birds of the wood rise chattering.
And now as she runs there is the bicker
Of a stream growing narrower in a trickle
And a splash and a flinging, it is water springing.
Now with her feet in deep moss Joan stands looking
Where on a bank a great white lady is lying
A fair smooth lady whose stomach swelling
Full breasts fine waist and long legs tapering
Are shadowed with grass-green streaks. The lady smiles
Lying naked. The sun stealing
Through the branches, her canopies, glorifies
The beautiful rich fat lady where she lies.
Never before in history
In a place so green and watery
Has lady's flesh and so divine a lady's as this is
With just such an admiring look as Joan's met with.
'Quite captive to the Lady of the Well-Spring'?
What nonsense, it is a thing
French ladies would say
In sophisticated conversation on a warm day.
I do not wish to rescue him, blurts Joan,
The lady lolls, Do you wish to go home?
No, says Joan, I should like to live
Here. Right, says the lady, you are my captive.
The child Joan fully sees the beauty her eye embraces
Do not think of her as one who loses.

THE QUEEN AND THE YOUNG PRINCESS

Mother, mother, let me go
There are so many things I wish to do.
My child, the time is not yet ripe
You are not yet ready for life.
But what is my life that is to come to be?
Much the same, child, as it has been for me.
But Mother you often say you have a headache
Because of the crown you wear for duty's sake.
So it is, so it is, a headache I have
And that is what you must grow up to carry to the grave.
But in between Mother do you not enjoy the pleasant weather
And to see the bluebottle and the soft feather?
Ah my child, that joy you speak of must be a pleasure
Of human stature, not the measure
Of animals', who have no glorious duty
To perform, no headache and so cannot see beauty.
Up, child, up, embrace the headache and the crown
Marred pleasure's best, shadow makes the sun strong.

A DREAM OF COMPARISON

After reading Book Ten of Paradise Lost.

Two ladies walked on the soft green grass
On the bank of a river by the sea
And one was Mary and the other Eve
And they talked philosophically.

'Oh to be Nothing,' said Eve, 'oh for a
Cessation of consciousness
With no more impressions beating in
Of various experiences.'

'How can Something envisage Nothing?' said Mary,
'Where's your philosophy gone?'
'Storm back through the gates of Birth,' cried Eve,
'Where were you before you were born?'

Mary laughed: 'I love Life,
I would fight to the death for it,
That's a feeling you say? I will find
A reason for it.'

They walked by the estuary,
Eve and the Virgin Mary,
And they talked until nightfall,
But the difference between them was radical.

MY HAT

Mother said if I wore this hat
I should be certain to get off with the right sort of chap
Well look where I am now, on a desert island

With so far as I can see no one at all on hand
I know what has happened though I suppose Mother wouldn't see
This hat being so strong has completely run away with me
I had the feeling it was beginning to happen the moment I put it on
What a moment that was as I rose up, I rose up like a flying swan
As strong as a swan too, why see how far my hat has flown me
  away
It took us a night to come and then a night and a day
And all the time the swan wing in my hat waved beautifully
Ah, I thought, How this hat becomes me.
First the sea was dark but then it was pale blue
And still the wing beat and we flew and we flew
A night and a day and a night, and by the old right way
Between the sun and the moon we flew until morning day.
It is always early morning here on this peculiar island
The green grass grows into the sea on the dipping land
Am I glad I am here? Yes, well, I am,
It's nice to be rid of Father, Mother and the young man
There's just one thing causes me a twinge of pain,
If I take my hat off, shall I find myself home again?
So in this early morning land I always wear my hat
Go home, you see, well I wouldn't run a risk like that.

THE ENGINE DRAIN

A Fenland Memory.

It was the mighty Engine Drain, the Engine Drain, the Engine
  Drain,
Down which the water went, the water went, the mighty waters
  of the inland sea.
But still in memory I see, the inland sea, the inland sea
That did reflect the summer sky, when it was summer time, of
  Cambridgeshire.

The sky was blue, the sea was blue, the inland sea, the inland sea,
All blue and flat and blue and flat it lay for all to see.
The trees stood up, the reeds stood too, and were reflected in the
    mere
As you might call that inland sea, you might have said it was a
    mere.
And in and out the branches all
The little birds did swoop and swing
Did swoop and swing and call
And oh it was a pretty thing to see them swoop and swing.
Oh ho the inland sea, the inland sea, the mighty mere that moved
    so prettily.

When winter came the water rose,
And rose and rose and rose and rose
And all about the cottage floors
It flowed and rose and flowed and rose
Till in their beds at night you'd see
Quite half afloat the midnight peasantry
That got their living hardily
And died of ripe old age rheumatically,
Oh it was quite surprising how
They'd live to ripe old age rheumatically.
It was because they early learnt
To put their boots on properly
While still in bed, while still in bed.
They learnt to put their boots on properly
Afloat in bed upon the inland sea.

And now I do remember how
Looking from shallow banks below
You'd see the little water-snakes
A-swimming to and fro,
So many little water-snakes
Careering round about

No man might stand to count them there
Careering in the pretty mere.

Oh it was merry in that day
To see the water-fowl play
Upon the inland sea,
Chip-chopping in the sea;
Or see them ride the water-race
In winter, till the winds in chase
Drove them ashore. Oh ho the wind upon the mere
It wound the waves in heaps and tossed the spray
That was half froze, upon the darkening day
Whipping the waters up till you might see
A mile away the whitecaps of the inland sea,
The whitecaps of the mere.

Ah me alas the day is past, is past and long ago
And no man living now may say he saw the waters flow,
All all are gone, the Engine Drain
Has took them to the cruel salt sea
And what is left behind?
A fertile flat and farming land,
A profitable farming land
Is what is left behind.
It took some time, as you might guess,
But not so long as you would guess,
A day or two, or two or three,
To take these waters to the sea
To take them to the Wash.

Why was it called the Engine Drain, the Engine Drain, the Engine
    Drain?
It was because the others were,
The other drains of Cambridgeshire,
Controlled by air, by windmills blowing there.

But oh this Engine was a force, a mighty engineering force,
It took the waters of the mere and brought them to the Wash,
It took them, did the Engine Drain, these waters of the inland sea,
And droppt 'em in the cruel salt sea,
The cruel salt sea.

SAINT ANTHONY AND THE ROSE OF LIFE

A Desert Vision.

A dark rose grew in the desert
A red and velvety flower
And opened her petals one by one
In the midnight hour.

Her leaves were a beautiful bright dark green
And this might only be seen
Because the full moon riding high
Threw a delicate beam.

The rose grew in a sand
Of a horrible gray yellow
For the moon that had made the red rose red
Made the sand sallow.

A strapping life heavy and bright
Bulged in the rose and her leaves
And up from the roots of the substantial plant
The bold drops ran like thieves.

Like burly thieves in a shadowy night
In a night of profound shades
They have carried aloft the colours of life
To flaunt in the deathly glades.

Oh rose oh leaves so much alive,
What are you doing here,
And why did you vanish at once away
In the light of a repentant tear?

ANGER'S FREEING POWER

I had a dream three walls stood up wherein a raven bird
Against the walls did beat himself and was not this absurd?

For sun and rain beat in that cell that had its fourth wall free
And daily blew the summer shower and the rain came presently

And all the pretty summer time and all the winter too
That foolish bird did beat himself till he was black and blue

Rouse up, rouse up, my raven bird, fly by the open wall
You make a prison of a place that is not one at all.

I took my raven by the hand, Oh come, I said, my Raven,
And I will take you by the hand and you shall fly to heaven.

But oh he sobbed and oh he sighed and in a fit he lay
Until two fellow ravens came and stood outside to say:

You wretched bird, conceited lump
You well deserve to pine and thump.

See now a wonder, mark it well
My bird rears up in angry spell,

Oh do I then? he says, and careless flies
O'er flattened wall at once to heaven's skies.

And in my dream I watched him go
And I was glad, I loved him so,

Yet when I woke my eyes were wet
To think Love had not freed my pet

Anger it was that won him hence
As only Anger taught him sense.

Often my tears fall in a shower
Because of Anger's freeing power.

FAFNIR AND THE KNIGHTS

In the quiet waters
Of the forest pool
Fafnir the dragon
His tongue will cool

His tongue will cool
And his muzzle dip
Until the soft waters lave
His muzzle tip

Happy simple creature
In his coat of mail
With a mild bright eye
And a waving tail

Happy the dragon
In the days expended
Before the time had come for dragons
To be hounded

Delivered in their simplicity
To the Knights of the Advancing Band
Who seeing the simple dragon
Must kill him out of hand

The time has not come yet
But must come soon
Meanwhile happy Fafnir
Take thy rest in the afternoon

Take thy rest
Fafnir while thou mayest
In the green grass
Where thou liest

Happy knowing not
In thy simplicity
That the knights have come
To do away with thee.

When thy body shall be torn
And thy lofty spirit
Broken into pieces
For a knight's merit

When thy lifeblood shall be spilt
And thy Being mild
In torment and dismay
To death beguiled

Fafnir, I shall say then,
Thou art better dead
For the knights have burnt thy grass
And thou couldst not have fed.

SONGE D'ATHALIE

From Racine.

It was a dream and shouldn't I bother about a dream?
But it goes on you know, tears me rather.
Of course I try to forget it but it will not let me.
Well it was on an extraordinarily dark night at midnight
My mother Queen Jezebel appeared suddenly before me
Looking just as she did the day she died, dressed grandly.
It was her pride you noticed, nothing she had gone through
    touched that
And she still had the look of being most carefully made up
She always made up a lot she didn't want people to know how old
    she was.
She spoke: Be warned my daughter, true girl to me, she said,
Do not suppose the cruel God of the Jews has finished with you,
I am come to weep your falling into his hands, my child.
With these appalling words my mother,
This ghost, leant over me stretching out her hands
And I stretched out my hands too to touch her
But what was it, oh this is horrible, what did I touch?
Nothing but the mangled flesh and the breaking bones
Of a body that the dogs tearing quarrelled over.

THE HOSTAGE

You hang at dawn, they said,
You've done nothing wrong but at dawn you will be hung.
You'll pass tonight in this cell
With Father Whatshisname. He'll look after you well.

There were two truckle beds in the room, on one sat Father W.,
Reclining against a bolster. The lady sat on the other.

I should like you to hear my confession, Father, I'm not of your
    persuasion
I'm a member of the Church of England, but on this occasion
I should like to talk to you, if you'll allow, nothing more,
Just a talk, not really a confession, but my heart is sore.
No, it's not that I have to die, that's the trouble, I've always
    wanted to
But it seems so despondent you know, ungracious too,

She sighed. Daughter, proceed,
Said the Father. I am here at your need.

Even as a child, said the lady, I recall in my pram
Wishing it was over and done with. Oh I am
Already at fault. Wonderful how 'bright' they keep,
I'd say of the other children, quite without rancour, then turn
    again to sleep.
Yet life is so beautiful. Oh the scenery.
Have you ever seen the sun getting up in the greenery
Of a summer day, in Norfolk say,
And the mild farm animals lumbering in the thistles.
Presently the Five-Thirty Milk in the station whistles,
You can hear the clank of the cans. In the wood
Trees dip to the stream, the fish rise up for food,
Snap, the old fly's caught. Et cetera. Oh it's busy,

Life bustles in the country, you know; it should be easy.
But I was outside of it, looking, finding no place,
No excuse at all for my distant wandering face.

When I came to London West-Eight, it was much the same
Oh the beautiful faces of others in the falling rain,
In the buses, no fuss there, no question they weren't at home,
Oh why should it only be I that was sent to roam?
I tell you, Father, I trod out the troughs of despair,
I'd rush out of doors in a fit, hurry, anywhere,
Kiss in my mind the darlings, beg them to stop . . .
Till the wind came up hard and blew my beauties off.
The wind blew hard. I snuffed it up and liked it,
Oh yes I liked it, that was the worst of it.

Of course I never dared form any close acquaintance.
Marriage? Out of the question. Well for instance
It might be infectious, this malaise of mine (an excuse?). Spread
That? I'd rather be dead.

But will the Lord forgive me? Is it wrong?
Will He forgive me do you think for not minding being hung,
Being glad it will soon be over,
Hoping he isn't the Ruler, the busy Lover,
Wishing to wake again, if I must at all,
As a vegetable leaning against a quiet wall,
Or an old stone, so old it was here before Man,
Or a flash in the fire that split our world from the sun?

I find nothing to instruct me in this in Holy Writ,
Said Father W., only, Remember life not to cling to it.

Well I don't you know, said the lady, then aware of something
    comical
Shot him a look that made him feel uncomfortable

Until he remembered she came from the British Isles,
Oh, he said, I've heard that's a place where nobody smiles.
But they do, said the lady, who loved her country, they laugh like
    anything
There is no one on earth who laughs so much about everything.

Well I see, said the Father, the case is complicated,
I will pray for you, Daughter, as I pray for all created
Meanwhile, since you want to die and have to, you may go on
    feeling elated.

AWAY, MELANCHOLY

> Away, melancholy,
> Away with it, let it go.
>
> Are not the trees green,
> The earth as green?
> Does not the wind blow,
> Fire leap and the rivers flow?
> Away melancholy.
>
> The ant is busy
> He carrieth his meat.
> All things hurry
> To be eaten or eat.
> Away, melancholy.
>
> Man, too, hurries,
> Eats, couples, buries,
> He is an animal also
> With a hey ho melancholy,
> Away with it, let it go.

Man of all creatures
Is superlative
(Away melancholy)
He of all creatures alone
Raiseth a stone
(Away melancholy)
Into the stone, the god
Pours what he knows of good
Calling, good, God.
Away melancholy, let it go.

Speak not to me of tears,
Tyranny, pox, wars,
Saying, Can God
Stone of man's thought, be good?

Say rather it is enough
That the stuffed
Stone of man's good, growing,
By man's called God.
Away, melancholy, let it go.

Man aspires
To good,
To love
Sighs;

Beaten, corrupted, dying
In his own blood lying
Yet heaves up an eye above
Cries, Love, love.
It is his virtue needs explaining,
Not his failing.

Away, melancholy,
Away with it, let it go.

DIDO'S FAREWELL TO AENEAS

From Virgil.

I have lived and followed my fate without flinching, followed it
    gladly
And now, not wholly unknown, I come to the end.
I built this famous city, I saw the walls rise,
As for my abominable brother, I don't think I've been too lenient.
Was I happy? Yes, at a price, I might have been happier
If our Dardanian Sailor had condescended to put in elsewhere.
Now she fell silent, turning her face to the pillow,
Then getting up quickly, the dagger in her hand,
I die unavenged, she cried, but I die as I choose,
Come Death, you know you must come when you're called
Although you're a god. And this way, and this way, I call you.

CHILDE ROLANDINE

Dark was the day for Childe Rolandine the artist
When she went to work as a secretary-typist
And as she worked she sang this song
Against oppression and the rule of wrong:

It is the privilege of the rich
To waste the time of the poor
To water with tears in secret
A tree that grows in secret
That bears fruit in secret
That ripened falls to the ground in secret
And manures the parent tree
Oh the wicked tree of hatred and the secret
The sap rising and the tears falling.

Likely also, sang the Childe, my soul will fry in hell
Because of this hatred, while in heaven my employer does well
And why should he not, exacerbating though he be but generous
Is it his fault I must work at a work that is tedious?
Oh heaven sweet heaven keep my thoughts in their night den
Do not let them by day be spoken.

But then she sang, Ah why not? tell all, speak, speak,
Silence is vanity, speak for the whole truth's sake.

And rising she took the bugle and put it to her lips, crying:
There is a Spirit feeds on our tears, I give him mine,
Mighty human feelings are his food
Passion and grief and joy his flesh and blood
That he may live and grow fat we daily die
This cropping One is our immortality.

Childe Rolandine bowed her head and in the evening
Drew the picture of the spirit from heaven.

THE JUNGLE HUSBAND

Dearest Evelyn, I often think of you
Out with the guns in the jungle stew
Yesterday I hittapotamus
I put the measurements down for you but they got lost in the fuss
It's not a good thing to drink out here
You know, I've practically given it up dear.
Tomorrow I am going alone a long way
Into the jungle. It is all gray
But green on top
Only sometimes when a tree has fallen
The sun comes down plop, it is quite appalling.

You never want to go in a jungle pool
In the hot sun, it would be the act of a fool
Because it's always full of anacondas, Evelyn, not looking ill-fed
I'll say. So no more now, from your loving husband, Wilfred.

'COME ON, COME BACK'

Incident in a future war.

Left by the ebbing tide of battle
On the field of Austerlitz
The girl soldier Vaudevue sits
Her fingers tap the ground, she is alone
At midnight in the moonlight she is sitting alone on a round flat
      stone.

Graded by the Memel Conference first
Of all humane exterminators
M.L.5.
Has left her just alive
Only her memory is dead for evermore.
She fears and cries, Ah me why am I here?
Sitting alone on a round flat stone on a hummock there.

Rising, staggering, over the ground she goes
Over the seeming miles of rutted meadow
To the margin of a lake
The sand beneath her feet
Is cold and damp and firm to the waves' beat.

Quickly – as a child, an idiot, as one without memory –
She strips her uniform off, strips, stands and plunges
Into the icy waters of the adorable lake.

On the surface of the water lies
A ribbon of white moonlight
The waters on either side of the moony track
Are black as her mind.
Her mind is as secret from her
As the water on which she swims,
As secret as profound as ominous.

Weeping bitterly for her ominous mind, her plight
Up the river of white moonlight she swims
Until a treacherous undercurrent
Seizing her in an icy-amorous embrace
Dives with her, swiftly severing
The waters which close above her head.

An enemy sentinel
Finding the abandoned clothes
Waits for the swimmer's return
('Come on, come back')
Waiting, whiling away the hour
Whittling a shepherd's pipe from the hollow reeds.

In the chill light of dawn
Ring out the pipe's wild notes
'Come on, come back.'

Vaudevue
In the swift and subtle current's close embrace
Sleeps on, stirs not, hears not the familiar tune
Favourite of all the troops of all the armies
Favourite of Vaudevue
For she had sung it too
Marching to Austerlitz,
'Come on, come back.'

Why are the clergy of the Church of England
Always altering the words of the prayers in the Prayer Book?
Cranmer's touch was surer than theirs, do they not respect him?
For instance last night in church I heard
(I italicize the interpolation)
'The Lord bless you and keep you *and all who are dear unto you*'
As the blessing is a congregational blessing and meant to be
This is questionable on theological grounds
But is it not offensive to the ear and also ludicrous?
That 'unto' is a particularly ripe piece of idiocy
Oh how offensive it is. I suppose we shall have next
'Lighten our darkness we beseech thee oh Lord *and the darkness of
     all who are dear unto us.*'
It seems a pity. Does Charity object to the objection?
Then I cry, and not for the first time to that smooth face
Charity, have pity.

I REMEMBER

It was my bridal night I remember,
An old man of seventy-three
I lay with my young bride in my arms,
A girl with t.b.
It was wartime, and overhead
The Germans were making a particularly heavy raid on
     Hampstead.
What rendered the confusion worse, perversely
Our bombers had chosen that moment to set out for Germany.
Harry, do they ever collide?
I do not think it has ever happened,
Oh my bride, my bride.

A mother slew her unborn babe
In a day of recent date
Because she did not wish him to be born in a world
Of murder and war and hate
'Oh why should I bear a babe from my womb
To be broke in pieces by the hydrogen bomb?'

I say this woman deserves little pity
That she was a fool and a murderess
Is a child's destiny to be contained by a mind
That signals only a lady in distress?

And why should human infancy be so superior
As to be too good to be born in this world?
Did she think it was an angel or a baa-lamb
That lay in her belly furled?

Oh the child is the young of its species
Alike with that noble, vile, curious and fierce
How foolish this poor mother to suppose
Her act told us aught that was not murderous

(As, item, That the arrogance of a half-baked mind
Breeds murder; makes us all unkind.)

THIS IS DISGRACEFUL
AND ABOMINABLE

Of all the disgraceful and abominable things
Making animals perform for the amusement of human beings is
Utterly disgraceful and abominable.

Animals are animals and have their nature
And that's enough, it is enough, leave it alone.

A disgraceful and abominable thing I saw in a French circus
A performing dog
Raised his back leg when he did not need to
He did not wish to relieve himself, he was made to raise his leg.
The people sniggered. Oh how disgraceful and abominable.
Weep for the disgrace, forbid the abomination.

The animals are cruelly trained,
How could patience do it, it would take too long, they are cruelly
      trained.
Lions leap through fire, it is offensive,
Elephants dance, it is offensive
That the dignified elephant should dance for fear of hot plates,
The lion leap or be punished.
And how can the animals be quartered or carted except cheaply?
Profit lays on the whip of punishment, money heats the prodding
      iron,
Cramps cages. Oh away with it, away with it, it is so disgraceful
      and abominable.
Weep the disgraces. Forbid the abominations.

GOD THE EATER

There is a god in whom I do not believe
Yet to this god my love stretches,
This god whom I do not believe in is
My whole life, my life and I am his.

Everything that I have of pleasure and pain
(Of pain, of bitter pain and men's contempt)
I give this god for him to feed upon
As he is my whole life and I am his.

When I am dead I hope that he will eat
Everything I have been and have not been
And crunch and feed upon it and grow fat
Eating my life all up as it is his.

GOD THE DRINKER

Porque Fue Sensible.

I like to see him drink the gash
I made with my own knife
And draw the blood out of my wrist
And drink my life.

Who is this One who drinks so deep?
His name is Death, He drinks asleep.

(She has taken the sweet knife far away,
The knife bleeds by night and day,
Night and day the blade drips,
I put the sweet knife to my lips.)

It was a god, he drank my health,
He came in shadows and by stealth.

WILL MAN EVER FACE FACT
AND NOT FEEL FLAT?

The rocks and trees in silence stood
To see where Man ran by,
A creature weak as this one is
What can he do but die?
But as they stood and scornful smiled
They heard an angel call:
'The tender creature needeth love,
He needeth love above all.'

This made the rocks and trees laugh more
Until they saw the force of it,
Saw Man disembowelling the earth
And killing because of it.

Ah then they found Man admirable
'But', said the angel, 'is he?'
And weeping cried, 'The need of love
Makes Man too busy,'

Then God said, 'You are wrong all,
The need of love is meant to call
Man to me, I am love, I,
If it does not, for lack of love he'll die.'

But then came a little wind sneaking along
That was older than all and infamously strong,
'Oh what an artistic animal is our little Man,'
Sneered the wind, 'It is wonderful how he can
Invent fairy stories about everything, pit pat,
Will he ever face fact and not feel flat?'

EVERY LOVELY LIMB'S A DESOLATION

I feel a mortal isolation
Wrap each lovely limb in desolation,
Sight, hearing, all
Suffer a fall.

I see the pretty fields and streams, I hear
Beasts calling and birds singing, oh not clear
But as a prisoner
Who in a train doth pass
And through the glass
Peer;
Ah me, so far away is joy, so near.

Break, break the glass, you say?
These thoughts are but a mood
Blow them away, go free?
They are my whole soul's food.

Ghost's food! Sepulchral aliment!
Thou sleekst in me Death's tegument
And so art bent
To do, and this I know.

Yet there are days, oh brief,
When thought's caught half-asleep
(Most merrily) and drowsing
Set in a meadow browsing.

Ah then, like summer breeze in lovely trees
That comes in little pants unequally,
Or like the little waves of summer seas
That push and fuss
In heaven knows what sort of busyness,

Idly, idly, my thoughts bring me to sleep,
On sunny summer day, to sleep. In sun
I fall asleep.

But I must wake and wake again in pain
Crying – to see where sun was once all dust and stain
As on a window pane –

All, all is isolation
And every lovely limb's a desolation.

A DREAM OF NOURISHMENT

I had a dream of nourishment
Against a breast
My infant face was presst
Ah me the *suffisance* I drew therefrom
What strength, what glory from that fattening fluid,
The fattening most
Was to my infant taste
For oh the sun of strength beat in my veins
And swelled me full, I lay in brightest sun
All ready to put forth, all bursting, all delight.

But in my dream the breast withdrew
In darkness I lay then
And thin,
Thin as a sheeted ghost
And I was famished,
Hankered for a dish
I thought, of blood, as in some classicist's
Old tale
To give me hue and substance, make me hale.

Oh breast, oh Best
That I held fast
Oh fattening draught
Timely repast
Quaffed, presst
And lost.

The breast was withdrawn violently
And oh the famishment for me.

THE AIRY CHRIST

After reading Dr Rieu's translation of St Mark's Gospel.

Who is this that comes in splendour, coming from the blazing
    East?
This is he we had not thought of, this is he the airy Christ.

Airy, in an airy manner in an airy parkland walking,
Others take him by the hand, lead him, do the talking.

But the Form, the airy One, frowns an airy frown,
What they say he knows must be, but he looks aloofly down,

Looks aloofly at his feet, looks aloofly at his hands,
Knows they must, as prophets say, nailèd be to wooden bands.

As he knows the words he sings, that he sings so happily
Must be changed to working laws, yet sings he ceaselessly.

Those who truly hear the voice, the words, the happy song,
Never shall need working laws to keep from doing wrong.

Deaf men will pretend sometimes they hear the song, the words,
And make excuse to sin extremely; this will be absurd.

Heed it not. Whatever foolish men may do the song is cried
For those who hear, and the sweet singer does not care that he was
    crucified.

For he does not wish that men should love him more than
    anything
Because he died; he only wishes they would hear him sing.

IT FILLED MY HEART WITH LOVE

*When I hold in my hand a soft and crushable animal, and feel the
fur beat for fear and the soft feather, I cannot feel unhappy.*

In his fur the animal rode, and in his fur he strove,
And oh it filled my heart my heart, it filled my heart with love.

I. AN AGNOSTIC

(of his religious friend)

He often gazes on the air
And sees quite plain what is not there
Peopling the wholesome void with horrid shapes
Which he manoeuvres in religious japes.
    And yet he is more gracious than I,
    He has such a gracious personality.

II. A RELIGIOUS MAN

(of his agnostic friend)

He says that religious thought and all our nerviness
Is because of the great shock it was for all of us
Long, long ago when animal turned human being
Which is more than enough to account for everything . . .
    And yet he is more gracious than I,
    He has such a gracious personality.

DEAR LITTLE SIRMIO

Catullus recollected.

Dear little Sirmio
Of all capes and islands
Wherever Neptune rides the coastal waters and the open sea
You really are the nicest.

How glad I am to see you again, how fondly I look at you.

No sooner had I left Bithynia – and what was the name of the
    other place?
And was safely at sea
I thought only of seeing you.

Really is anything nicer
After working hard and being thoroughly worried
Than to leave it all behind and set out for home
Dear old home and one's own comfortable bed?

Even if one wears oneself out paying for them.

'GREAT UNAFFECTED VAMPIRES
AND THE MOON'

It was a graveyard scene. The crescent moon
Performed a devil's purpose for she shewed
The earth a-heap where smooth it should have lain;
And in and out the tombs great witches' cats
Played tig-a-tag and sang harmoniously.
Beneath the deathly slopes the palings stood
Catching the moonlight on their painted sides,
Beyond, the waters of a mighty lake
Stretching five furlongs at its fullest length
Lay as a looking-glass, framed in a growth
Of leafless willows; all its middle part
Was open to the sky, and there I saw
Embosomed in the lake together lie
Great unaffected vampires and the moon.
A Christian crescent never would have lent
Unchristian monsters such close company
And so I say she was no heavenly light
But devil's in that business manifest
And as the vampires seemed quite unaware
I thought she'd lost her soul for nothing lying there.

THE CELTS

I think of the Celts as rather a whining lady
Who was beautiful once but is not so much so now
She is not very loving, but there is one thing she loves
It is her grievance which she hugs and takes out walking.

The Celtic lady likes fighting very much for freedom
But when she has got it she is a proper tyrant
Nobody likes her much when she is governing.

The Celtic lady is not very widely popular
But the English love her oh they love her very much
Especially when the Celtic lady is Irish they love her
Which is odd as she hates them then more than anyone else.
When she's Welsh the English stupidly associate her chiefly
With national hats, eisteddfods and Old Age Pensions.
(They don't think of her at all when she is Scotch, it is rather a
    problem.)

Oh the Celtic lady when she's Irish is the one for me
Oh she is so witty and wild, my word witty,
And flashing and spiteful this Celtic lady we love
All the same she is not so beautiful as she was.

THE PASSING CLOUD

From The Royal Bethlehem Hospital.

I thought as I lay on my bed one night, I am only a passing cloud
And I wiped the tear from my sorrowful eye and merrily cried
    aloud
Oh the love of the Lord is a fearful thing and the love of the Lord
    is mine
And what do I care for the sins of men and the tears of our guilty
    time
I will sail my cloud in the bright blue sky, in the bright blue sky I
    sail
And I look at the sea so merrily swung in the path of the Arctic
    whale
On the tropic belt of the uttermost wild the sea rings a merry peal
And the fish leaps up and the sharks pursue in Creation's happy reel
Oh I dance on my cloud and I cry aloud to the careless creative
    gust
That made us all and made the fish and the ocean that holds them
    fast
Hurrah hurrah for the grand old heavenly gusty creator Lord
Who said to Job, Don't bother me son, I'll do as I please my word.
Oh never was happiness like to mine as I pelt along on my cloud
In the sky-blue path of the high winds' breath, no wonder I cry
    aloud
With joy I cried and my cheeks were wet and the air was a singing
    space
And I thought as we shot to the upper reach, My lord, it's a lick of
    a pace.
When we swept out of sight of the troublesome earth, was I afraid,
    oh no,
I was glad to see the parochial thing pack up its traps and go
And now I go round and round I go in the merry abyss of the sky
Piercing the grand primaeval dust of the stars in their infancy

I tunnel, I burrow, I offer my dust as a dust for creation's choice
And in the ding-dong of the universe I pipe my innocent voice
I pipe my innocent voice I pipe, I pipe and I also sing
Till I'd sung too loud and woke myself up and that is another
    thing,
Oh I woke with a bump and they brought me here to
    Bethlehem's Royal precincts
And do I care? Not I, not I, I have shed all careful instincts,
I will laugh and sing, or be dumb if they please, and await at the
    Lord's discretion
The day I'll be one, as one I'll be, in an infinite regression
One, ha ha, with a merry ha ha, skip the fish and amoeba where
    are we now?
We are very far out, in a rarified place, with the thin thin dust in a
    giddy chase,
The dust of Continuous Creation, and how is that for
    identification?
You'll like it; you must, you know,
That merry dust does jig so.

LOIN DE L'ÊTRE

You don't look at all well, quite loin de l'être in fact
Poor pale-face what's the matter, don't they know?
Oh they don't know, but still I don't feel well
Nor ever shall, my name is *Loin de l'Être*.

They stood on the empty terrace above the precipice
When this conversation took place
Between the affectionate but exasperated friend
And the invalid. It is not possible to be
Ill and merry, poor *Loin de l'Être* sighed
And forced a smile, but oh she was so tired.
So tired, called Echo, so tired.

Now pull yourself together, cried the friend
Together cried Echo,
I must leave you now for a tick, she said
Mind you don't get edgy looking at the precipice.
The lovely invalid sighed, Loin de l'être,
And Echo taking the form of a handsome young man
Cried, *Loin de l'Être* and took her away with him.

MY CAT MAJOR

Major is a fine cat
What is he at?
He hunts birds in the hydrangea
And in the tree
Major was ever a ranger
He ranges where no one can see.

Sometimes he goes up to the attic
With a hooped back
His paws hit the iron rungs
Of the ladder in a quick kick
How can this be done?
It is a knack.

Oh Major is a fine cat
He walks cleverly
And what is he at, my fine cat?
No one can see.

PARENTS

Parents who barely can afford it
Should not send their children to public schools ill will reward it
That skimping and saving and giving up
That seems so unselfish will buy you a pup
Oh what an ugly biting bow-wow
Well Colonel, how does it go now?
Your son aged twenty-two wears a glittering blazer
His conversation about ponds and ducks, oh happy fool,
Is interrupted to speak of his school
As if at fault he'd allowed
Momentarily that pond to draw him from being proud.
Ah, so hardly won through to it, Colonel,
Is to attach too much importance to it.
But he's saved; ponds, duck, fish in dark water
Have a tight hold of him. It is your daughter
Colonel, who is wholly corrupted.
Women when they are snobbish do not loaf
Look at fish, are not oafish
But are persistently mercenary, cold, scheming and calculating,
This in a young girl is revolting.
Oh beautiful brave mother, the wife of the colonel,
How could you allow your young daughter to become aware of
    the scheming?
If you had not, it might have stayed a mere dreaming
Of palaces and princes, girlish at worst.
Oh to become sensible about social advance at seventeen is to be
    lost.

TO A LADY IN A TRAIN

She is not Indian, she's ill
'Tis Death hath darkened that pale cheek of hers,
No sun of Indian summer in a trench
Of climate tropical hath made her brown
That was so pale and fair, a northern girl.

Now look more close. That colour's gray not brown
Death certainly hath hold of her, his fingers
Stop up the blood to blacken where it lingers
Death hath her now till gray to black shall turn.

Ah then her soul now ru ffling up befeathered
In practice for the flight when Death hath done
Flying shall mock all those who stay at home
And cry: Begone,
Cast off from fleshy station,
Death untethered,
To heaven flown.

Seeing her now this day so soon to go
I would go too
And I say true,

If being Indian not ill had put it on
I should not so much envy her complexion.

ADELAIDE ABNER

Adelaide Abner is cruel
She is grown into a cruel beast
She does not ask me to her parties now
She wants to be first at the feast.

But oh the parties were so beautiful
And I did not monopolize the faces
I was only happy to be delivered for a time
From silence.

Silence at depth is cold
It is misty and full of pain
And because of Adelaide Abner's cruelty
I am in silence again.

Then the girl knelt down and repented
Of what she had said about Adelaide,
Was I a true friend? she wondered,
Yes, I was a true friend, she said.

I was looking for a venial motive,
Vanity might change like the weather,
But oh her heart is cold
And so it is goodbye for ever.

THE ENGLISH

Many of the English,
The intelligent English,
Of the Arts, the Professions and the Upper Middle Classes,
Are under-cover men,
But what is under the cover
(That was original)
Died; now they are corpse-carriers.
It is not noticeable, but be careful,
They are infective.

KING HAMLET'S GHOST

'It would be spoke to.'

Poor noble Ghost that comes from place of pain
Of so much pain and foul and fiery,
To tread again in mournful armour clad
Thy soft gray fields upon a winter's night
Thou wouldst be spoke to, for unless one speaks
Thou canst not; *must* be spoke to then or go
Unheard, uncomforted to Misery.
I pity thy royal brow, thy temper too,
Thy crownèd brow and the sharp savagery
That, when thy son had spoke, found out in words
A long expression of revengefulness,
'Kill, kill the murderers.' All those who go
In midnight fields of melancholy thought
Where friends pass distantly and do not speak
May cry 'Kill, kill' for they are murdered too
As set upon by Silence and quite killed.
'Speak, speak to me' they cry, 'I would be spoke to'
But oh the friends speak not, they have too much to do.

AT SCHOOL

A Paolo and Francesca situation but more hopeful, say in Purgatory.

At school I always walk with Elwyn
Walk with Elwyn all the day
Oh my darling darling Elwyn
We shall never go away.

This school is a most curious place
Everything happens faintly
And the other boys and girls who are here
We cannot see distinctly.

All the day I walk with Elwyn
And sometimes we also ride
Both of us would really always
Rather be outside.

Most I like to ride with Elwyn
In the early morning sky
Under the solitary mosses
That hang from the trees awry.

The wind blows cold then
And the wind comes to the dawn
And we ride silently
And kiss as we ride down.

Oh my darling darling Elwyn
Oh what a sloppy love is ours
Oh how this sloppy love sustains me
When we come back to the school bars.

There are bars round this school
And inside the lights are always burning bright
And yet there are shadows
That belong rather to the night than to the light.

Oh my darling darling Elwyn
Why is there this dusty heat in this closed school?
All the radiators must be turned full on
Surely that is against the rules?

Hold my hand as we run down the long corridors
Arched over with tombs
We are underground now a long way
Look out, we are getting close to the boiler room.

We are not driven harshly to the lessons you know
That go on under the electric lights
That go on persistently, patiently you might say,
They do not mind if we are not very bright.

Open this door quick, Elwyn, it is break-time
And if we ride quickly we can come to the sea-pool
And swim; will not that be a nice thing to do?
Oh my darling do not look so sorrowful.

Oh why do we cry so much
Why do we not go to some place that is nice?
Why do we only stand close
And lick the tears from each other's eyes?

Darling, my darling
You are with me in the school and in the dead trees' glade
If you were not with me
I should be afraid.

Fear not the ragged dawn skies
Fear not the heat of the boiler room
Fear not the sky where it flies
The jagged clouds in their rusty colour.

Do not tell me not to cry my love
The tears run down your face too
There is still half an hour left
Can we not think of something to do?

There goes the beastly bell
Tolling us to lessons
If I do not like this place much
That bell is the chief reason.

Oh darling Elwyn love
Our tears fall down together
It is because of the place we're in
And because of the weather.

CAN IT BE?

Can it be, can it be
That beasts are of various bravery,
Some brave by nature, some not at all,
Some trying to be against a fall?

I saw a cat. Beside a lily tank,
Paved level with the grass, she stood, this cat,
Considering her leap.
Three times she backed for jumping, gathered tight
(So tight, thought landed her already over)
And did not jump. And then,
After a pause, as scolding humanly
'Not nervy, eh? We'll see.'
She jumped. And what a jump that was!
Quite twice as long
And high
As it need be,
Now why
Did this cat jump at all, so force herself?
There was a path around the tank,
She could have walked.

Can it be, can it be
That beasts are of various bravery,
Some simply brave, some not, some taking thought
(Most curiously) to cast themselves aloft?

THE OLD SWEET DOVE OF WIVETON

'Twas the voice of the sweet dove
I heard him move
I heard him cry
Love, love.

High in the chestnut tree
Is the nest of the old dove
And there he sits solitary
Crying, Love, love.

The gray of this heavy day
Makes the green of the trees' leaves and the grass brighter
And the flowers of the chestnut tree whiter
And whiter the flowers of the high cow-parsley.

So still is the air
So heavy the sky
You can hear the splash
Of the water falling from the green grass
As Red and Honey push by,
The old dogs,
Gone away, gone hunting by the marsh bogs.

Happy the retriever dogs in their pursuit
Happy in bog-mud the busy foot.

Now all is silent, it is silent again
In the sombre day and the beginning soft rain
It is a silence made more actual
By the moan from the high tree that is occasional,

Where in his nest above
Still sits the old dove,
Murmuring solitary
Crying for pain,
Crying most melancholy
Again and again.

THE PAST

People who are always praising the past
And especially the times of faith as best
Ought to go and live in the Middle Ages
And be burnt at the stake as witches and sages.

THE SINGING CAT

It was a little captive cat
 Upon a crowded train
His mistress takes him from his box
 To ease his fretful pain.

She holds him tight upon her knee
 The graceful animal
And all the people look at him
 He is so beautiful.

But oh he pricks and oh he prods
    And turns upon her knee
Then lifteth up his innocent voice
    In plaintive melody.

He lifteth up his innocent voice
    He lifteth up, he singeth
And to each human countenance
    A smile of grace he bringeth.

He lifteth up his innocent paw
    Upon her breast he clingeth
And everybody cries, Behold
    The cat, the cat that singeth.

He lifteth up his innocent voice
    He lifteth up, he singeth
And all the people warm themselves
    In the love his beauty bringeth.

LONGING FOR DEATH
BECAUSE OF FEEBLENESS

Oh would that I were a reliable spirit careering around
Congenially employed and no longer by *feebleness* bound
Oh who would not leave the flesh to become a reliable spirit
Possibly travelling far and acquiring merit.

MY HEART GOES OUT

My heart goes out to my Creator in love
Who gave me Death, as end and remedy.
All living creatures come to quiet Death
For him to eat up their activity
And give them nothing, which is what they want although
When they are living they do not think so.

LOOK!

I am becalmed in a deep sea
And give signals, but they are not answered
And yet I see ships in the distance
And give signals, but they do not answer.

Am I a pariah ship, or a leper
To be shunned reasonably?
Or did I commit a crime long ago
And have forgotten, but they remember?

Into the dark night to darker I move
And the lights of the ships are not seen now
But instead there is a phosphorescence from the water.
That light shines, and now I see

Low down, as I bend my hand in the water
A fish so transparent in his inner organs
That I know he comes from the earthquake bed
Five miles below where I sail, I sail.

All his viscera are transparent, his eyes globule on stalks,
Is he dead? Or alive and only languid? Now
Into my hand he comes, the travelling creature,

Not from the sea-bed only but from the generations,
Faint because of the lighter pressure,
Fainting, a long fish, stretched out.

So we meet, and for a moment
I forget my solitariness
But then I should like to show him,
And who shall I show him to?

WHO IS THIS WHO HOWLS AND MUTTERS?

Who is this that howls and mutters?
It is the Muse, each word she utters
Is thrown against a shuttered door
And very soon she'll speak no more.

Cry louder, Muse, make much more noise
The world is full of rattling toys
I thought she'd say, Why should I then?
I have spoke low to better men
But oh she did not speak at all but went away
And now I search for her by night and day.

Night and day I seek my Muse
Seek the one I did abuse
She had so sweet a face, so sweet a voice
But oh she did not make sufficient noise.

False plea. I did not listen then
That listen now and listen now in vain.

And still the tale of talent murdered
Untimely and untimely buried
Works in my soul. Forgive me, Lord, I cry
Who only makest Muses howl and sigh
Thou, Lord, repent and give her back to me
Weeping uncomforted, Lord have pity.

He did repent. I have her now again
Howling much worse, and oh the door is open.

MAGNA EST VERITAS

With my looks I am bound to look simple or fast I would rather
    look simple
So I wear a tall hat on the back of my head that is rather a temple
And I walk rather queerly and comb my long hair
And people say, Don't bother about her.
So in my time I have picked up a good many facts,
Rather more than the people do who wear smart hats
And I do not deceive because I am rather simple too
And although I collect facts I do not always know what they
    amount to.
I regard them as a contribution to almighty Truth, magna est
    veritas et praevalebit,
Agreeing with that Latin writer, Great is Truth and will prevail in
    a bit.

THE LIGHT OF LIFE

Put out that Light,
Put out that bright Light,
Let darkness fall.

Put out that Day,
It is the time for nightfall.

IN THE PARK

Walking one day in the park in winter
I heard two silvered gentlemen talking,
Two old friends, elderly, walking, talking
There by the silver lake mid-pooled black in winter.

'Pray for the Mute who have no word to say,'
Cried the one old gentleman, 'Not because they are dumb,
But they are weak. And the weak thoughts beating in the brain
Generate a sort of heat, yet cannot speak.
Thoughts that are bound without sound
In the tomb of the brain's room, wound. Pray for the Mute.'

'But' (said his friend), 'see how they swim
Free in the element best loved, so wet; yet breathe
As a visitor to the air come; plunge then, rejoicing more,
Having left it briefly for the visited shore, to come
Home to the wet
Windings that are yet
Best loved though familiar; and oh so right the wet
Stream and the wave; he is their pet.'

Finished, the mild friend
Smiled, put aside his well-tuned hearing instrument
And it seemed
The happiness he spoke of
Irradiated all his members, and his heart
Barked with delight to stress
So much another's happiness.

But which other's? The sombre first
Speaker reversed
The happy moment; cried again
(Mousing for pain) 'Pray for the Mute' (a tear drops)
'They are like the brute.'

Struck by the shout
That he may not know what it's about
The deaf friend again
Up-ends his hearing instrument to relieve the strain.
What? Oh shock, ' "Pray for the Mute"?
I thought you said the newt.'

Now which is Christianer pray, of these old friends, the one
        who will say
For pain's sake pray, pray; or the deaf other that rejoices
So much that the cool amphibian
Shall have his happiness, all things rejoicing with him?

But wait; the first speaker now, the old sombre one,
Is penetrated quite by his friend's sun
And, 'Oh blessed you,' he cries, 'to show
So in simplicity what is true.'
All his face is suffused with happy tears and as he weeps he sings
        a happy song,
Happier even than his friend's song was, righting the wrong.
So two, better than one, finally strike truth in his happy song:

'Praise,' cries the weeping softened one, 'Not pray, praise,
    all men,
Praise is the best prayer, the least self's there, that least's
    release.'

EVANGELIE
or
THE FIGURE OF LITERARY CORRUPTION,
SEEKING GLORY NOT TRUTH

Wicked and corrupt
Was Evangelie
And the corruption came out of her
On to me.

Corruptest and most wicked
Of creatures,
Can I forget a word she said
Or her features?

Lord, cleanse me of the corruption
Of Evangelie,
And of my feelings for her,
That I may wear again the garment of whiteness,
And the fair crown in my hair.

JUMBO

Jumbo, Jumbo, Jumbo darling, Jumbo come to Mother.
But Jumbo wouldn't, he was a dog who simply wouldn't bother
An ugly beast he was with drooping guts and filthy skin,
It was quite wonderful how 'mother' loved the ugly thing.

THE CHOOSERS

Who shall we send to fetch him away
This young-man Author of the Month of May?
We will send Mr Puff to fetch him away,
We are the Choosers and stand in the way.

Oh we are the Choosers, what we say goes.
Does Puff know this? Yes, Puff knows.
Hey ho what a merry game,
It is as if we were still in Pop, it is the same.

With a hey-ho and a yah
No, we will not have So-and-So
Because we do not like his hat or his Ma.

Outside of this eclectic and up-to-date circle
Slink the sleek Great Ones, and you know
They may go and not care a particle
Because the Angel of Posterity has chosen them
And the Choosers will not be known then,
All the same it is a shame to treat them so.

Let Posterity-Time come
Quick and Choosers be dumb.

Oh why does England cherish her arts in this wise,
Picking inferiorly with grafted eyes?
It is because it is like the school they never forget,
So-and-so must be the driven out one, this the pet.

THE OCCASIONAL YARROW

It was a mile of greenest grass
Whereon a little stream did pass,
    The Occasional Yarrow

Only in every seventh year
Did this pretty stream appear,
    The Occasional Yarrow

Wading and warbling in its beds
Of grass decked out with daisy heads,
    The Occasional Yarrow

There in my seventh year, and this sweet stream's,
I wandered happily (as happy gleams
    The Occasional Yarrow).

Though now to memory alone
I can call up thy lovely form,
    Occasional Yarrow

I still do bless thy Seventh days
Bless thy sweet name and all who praise
    The Occasional Yarrow.

THE SORROWFUL GIRL

Muriel, Muriel, marry me Muriel,
And I will comfort you as well
And bring life to your pale hair
And your languid air.

Ah then I shall not be I, for I am here
With my languid air and lifeless hair
And I do not feel cold or heat
I am imprisoned and do not need to be freed
My prison is my sorrowful mind
And I do not wish to leave it behind
Wake me not, leave me here, leave me alone
I am as God made me, a sorrowful one.

And singing she sang, I am sorrowful, sorrowful
And because I am sorrowful I am beautiful.

Her lover has left her and gone angrily off
He speaks of her only to laugh and to scoff
Pretending he only wanted to marry her for her money
Intending to prove his thoughts were not moony
With love, or any such stuff,
That he is not such a fool as to have had a rebuff.

A pale light-moon-white lily romantic girl-of-a-lover
With nothing to her name but two thousand pounds in Old
    Consols, who will have her?
Is the burden of the anger of this churl and of his troubles.

But ever there came from far away
Growing fainter with the passing day
The sorrowful song on the sorrowful air
Of the languid girl with the lifeless hair
Singing: Oh I am sorrowful, sorrowful, sorrowful
And because I am sorrowful I am beautiful.

THE STARLING

I will never leave you darling
To be eaten by the starling
For I love you more than ever
In the wet and stormy weather.

Thus to the husband sang the wife
That loved him more than his own life
Oh at these words the husband felt
Each hair rise separate upon his icy pelt.

He let himself down from out his room
He went upon the ancient mountain
And there he quite forgot his gloom
As he trod the torrent's icy fountain.

Cold, cold, icy cold,
Cold, cold, cold I am,
Cold has no place in my wife's warm thought
There she will have me cradled and wraught.
Oh nothing, nothing, nothing I
He cried, that in her thinking does not lie.

Then he doffed his clothes and quickly froze
In the ice of the ancient mountain-side
And there in an icy happy doze
He doth for evermore abide.

Down in the valley waits the wife
That loved him more than his own life
And still she sings, in hope to lure
Him to her side again, Be very sure

I will never leave you darling
To be eaten by the starling
For I love you more than ever
In the wet and stormy weather.

DIE LORELEI

An antique story comes to me
And fills me with anxiety,
I wonder why I fear so much
What surely has no modern touch?

It is of Germany it speaks,
One evening time; the mountain peaks
Are in the sun, but the old Rhine
Flows secretly and does not shine.

There, on a rock majestical,
A girl with smile equivocal,
Painted, young and damned and fair,
Sits and combs her yellow hair.

With a yellow comb she combs it,
Sings a song, and sometimes moans it,
That has a most peculiar turn,
It makes the heart and belly burn.

The sailor sailing, hearing it
Falls at once into a fit,
He does not see the rocky race,
His eyes are looking for a face.

The boat strikes hard, as she must do,
And down she goes, and he goes too.
This story brings me so much grief
I know not how to find relief.

Lurks there some meaning underneath?

FAREWELL

Farewell dear friends
I loved you so much
But now I must leave you
And spread over me the dust

Fair life fare well
Fare never ill
Far I go now
And say, Farewell.

Farewell dear world
With the waters around you curled
And the grass on your breast
I loved you best.

Farewell fish and insect
Bird, animal, swift mover
Grim reptile as well
I was your approver.

Wide sky, farewell,
Sun, moon, stars in places
Farewell all fair universes
In far places.

Ding dong, ding dong
As a bell is rung,
Sing ding dong farewell
As a sweet bell.

THOUGHTS ABOUT THE PERSON
FROM PORLOCK

Coleridge received the Person from Porlock
And ever after called him a curse,
Then why did he hurry to let him in?
He could have hid in the house.

It was not right of Coleridge in fact it was wrong
(But often we all do wrong)
As the truth is I think he was already stuck
With Kubla Khan.

He was weeping and wailing: I am finished, finished,
I shall never write another word of it,
When along comes the Person from Porlock
And takes the blame for it.

It was not right, it was wrong,
But often we all do wrong.

*

May we inquire the name of the Person from Porlock?
Why, Porson, didn't you know?
He lived at the bottom of Porlock Hill
So had a long way to go,

He wasn't much in the social sense
Though his grandmother was a Warlock,
One of the Rutlandshire ones I fancy
And nothing to do with Porlock,

And he lived at the bottom of the hill as I said
And had a cat named Flo,
And had a cat named Flo.

I long for the Person from Porlock
To bring my thoughts to an end,
I am becoming impatient to see him
I think of him as a friend,

Often I look out of the window
Often I run to the gate
I think, He will come this evening,
I think it is rather late.

I am hungry to be interrupted
For ever and ever amen
O Person from Porlock come quickly
And bring my thoughts to an end.

*

I felicitate the people who have a Person from Porlock
To break up everything and throw it away
Because then there will be nothing to keep them
And they need not stay.

*

Why do they grumble so much?
He comes like a benison
They should be glad he has not forgotten them
They might have had to go on.

*

These thoughts are depressing I know. They are depressing,
I wish I was more cheerful, it is more pleasant,
Also it is a duty, we should smile as well as submitting
To the purpose of One Above who is experimenting
With various mixtures of human character which goes best,
All is interesting for him it is exciting, but not for us.
There I go again. Smile, smile, and get some work to do
Then you will be practically unconscious without positively
     having to go.

THE FROG PRINCE

I am a frog
I live under a spell
I live at the bottom
Of a green well

And here I must wait
Until a maiden places me
On her royal pillow
And kisses me
In her father's palace.

The story is familiar
Everybody knows it well
But do other enchanted people feel as nervous
As I do? The stories do not tell,

Ask if they will be happier
When the changes come
As already they are fairly happy
In a frog's doom?

I have been a frog now
For a hundred years
And in all this time
I have not shed many tears,

I am happy, I like the life,
Can swim for many a mile
(When I have hopped to the river)
And am for ever agile.

And the quietness,
Yes, I like to be quiet
I am habituated
To a quiet life,

But always when I think these thoughts
As I sit in my well
Another thought comes to me and says:
It is part of the spell

To be happy
To work up contentment
To make much of being a frog
To fear disenchantment

Says, It will be *heavenly*
To be set free,
Cries, *Heavenly* the girl who disenchants
And the royal times, *heavenly*,
And I think it will be.

Come then, royal girl and royal times,
Come quickly,
I can be happy until you come
But I cannot be heavenly,
Only disenchanted people
Can be heavenly.

A HOUSE OF MERCY

It was a house of female habitation,
Two ladies fair inhabited the house,
And they were brave. For although Fear knocked loud
Upon the door, and said he must come in,
They did not let him in.

There were also two feeble babes, two girls,
That Mrs S. had by her husband had,
He soon left them and went away to sea,
Nor sent them money, nor came home again
Except to borrow back
Her Naval Officer's Wife's Allowance from Mrs S.
Who gave it him at once, she thought she should.

There was also the ladies' aunt
And babes' great aunt, a Mrs Martha Hearn Clode,
And she was elderly.
These ladies put their money all together
And so we lived.

I was the younger of the feeble babes
And when I was a child my mother died
And later Great Aunt Martha Hearn Clode died
And later still my sister went away.

Now I am old I tend my mother's sister
The noble aunt who so long tended us,
Faithful and True her name is. Tranquil.
Also Sardonic. And I tend the house.

It is a house of female habitation
A house expecting strength as it is strong
A house of aristocratic mould that looks apart
When tears fall; counts despair
Derisory. Yet it has kept us well. For all its faults,
If they are faults, of sternness and reserve,
It is a Being of warmth I think; at heart
A house of mercy.

AVONDALE

How sweet the birds of Avondale
Of Avondale, of Avondale,
How sweet the birds of Avondale
Do swoop and swing and call.

The children too of Avondale,
Of Avondale, of Avondale,
The boys and girls of Avondale
Do swoop and swing and call,

And all the little cats and dogs,
Of Avondale, of Avondale,
In their own way in Avondale
Do swoop and swing and call,

And oh it is a pleasant sight
It is a very pleasant sight
To see the creatures so delight
To swoop and swing and call,
In Avondale, in Avondale,
To see them swoop and call.

SCORPION

'This night shall thy soul be required of thee'
My soul is never required of *me*
It always has to be somebody else of course
Will my soul be required of me tonight perhaps?

(I often wonder what it will be like
To have one's soul required of one
But all I can think of is the Out-Patients' Department –
'Are you Mrs Briggs, dear?'
No, I am Scorpion.)

I should like my soul to be required of me, so as
To waft over grass till it comes to the blue sea
I am very fond of grass, I always have been, but there must
Be no cow, person or house to be seen.

Sea and *grass* must be quite empty
Other souls can find somewhere *else*.

O Lord God please come
And require the soul of thy Scorpion

Scorpion so wishes to be gone.

SEYMOUR AND CHANTELLE
or
UN PEU DE VICE

In memory of A. Swinburne and Mary Gordon.

Pull my arm back, Seymour,
Like the boys do,
Oh Seymour, the pain, the pain,
Still more then, do.
I am thy schoolboy friend, now I
Am not Chantelle any more but mi.
Say 'sweet mi', 'my sweet mi'. Oh the pain, the pain,
Kiss me and I will kiss you again.

Tell me, Seymour, when they ... when ...
Does it hurt as much as this
And this and this? Ah what pain.
When I do so I feel
How very painful it is for you,
No I will, so, again and again,
Now stuff the dockleaves in your mouth
And bite the pain.

Seymour, when you hold me so tight it hurts
I feel my ribs break and the blood spurt,

Oh what heaven, what bliss,
Will you kiss me, if I give you this
Kiss, and this and this? Like this?

Seymour, this morning Nanny swished me so hard
(Because I told her she had the face
Of an antediluvian animal that had
Become extinct because of being so wet)
She broke her hair-brush. What bliss.
No, don't stop me now with a kiss, oh God it was pain-
Ful, I could not stop crying.

Oh darling, what heaven, how did you think
Of doing that? You are my sweetest angel of a
Little cousin, and your tears
Are as nice as the sea, as icy and salt as it is.

HOW DO YOU SEE?

How do you see the Holy Spirit of God?
I see him as the holy spirit of good,
But I do not think we should talk about spirits, I think
We should call good, good.

But it is a beautiful idea, is it not?
And productive of good?

Yes, that is the problem, it is productive of good,
As Christianity now is productive of good,
So that a person who does not believe the Christian faith
Feels he must keep silent, in case good suffers,
In case what good there is in the world diminishes.

But must we allow good to be hitched to a lie,
A beautiful cruel lie, a beautiful fairy story,
A beautiful idea, made up in a loving moment?

Yes, it is a beautiful idea, one of the most
Beautiful ideas Christianity has ever had,
This idea of the Spirit of God, the Holy Ghost,
My heart goes out to this beautiful Holy Ghost,
He is so beautifully inhuman, he is like the fresh air.
They represent him as a bird, I dislike that,
A bird is parochial to our world, rooted as we are
In pain and cruelty. Better the fresh air.

But before we take a Christian idea to alter it
We should look what the idea is, we should read in their books
Of holy instruction what the Christians say. What do they say
Of the beautiful Holy Ghost? They say

That the beautiful Holy Ghost brooded on chaos
And chaos gave birth to form. As this we cannot know
It can only be beautiful if told as a fairy story,
Told as a fact it is harmful, for it is not a fact.

But it is a beautiful fairy story. I feel so much
The pleasure of the bird on the dark and powerful waters,
And here I like to think of him as a bird, I like to feel
The masterful bird's great pleasure in his breast
Touching the water. Like! Like! What else do they say?

Oh I know we must put away the beautiful fairy stories
And learn to be good in a dull way without enchantment,
Yes, we must. What else do they say? They say

That the beautiful Holy Spirit burning intensely,
Alight as never was anything in this world alight,
Inspired the scriptures. But they are wrong,

Often the scriptures are wrong. For I see the Pope
Has forbidden the verse in Mark ever to be discussed again
And I see a doctor of Catholic divinity saying
That some verses in the New Testament are pious forgeries
Interpolated by eager clerks avid for good.

Ah good, what is good, is it good
To leave in scripture the spurious verses and not print
A footnote to say they are spurious, an erratum slip?

And the penal sentences of Christ: He that believeth
And is baptized shall be saved, he that believeth not
Shall be damned. Depart from me ye cursed into everlasting fire
Prepared for the devil and his angels. And then
Saddest of all the words in scripture, the words,
They went away into everlasting punishment. Is this good?

Yes, nowadays certainly it is very necessary before we take
The ideas of Christianity, the words of our Lord,
To make them good, when often they are not very good,
To see what the ideas are and the words; to look at them.

Does the beautiful Holy Ghost endorse the doctrine of eternal hell?
Love cruelty, enjoin the sweet comforts of religion?
Oh yes, Christianity, yes, he must do this
For he is your God, and in your books

You say he informs, gives form, gives life, instructs.
Instructs, that is the bitterest part. For what does he instruct
As to the dreadful bargain, that God would take and offer
The death of the Son to buy our faults away,
The faults of the faulty creatures of the Trinity?
Oh Christianity, instructed by the Holy Ghost,
What do you mean? As to Christ, what do you mean?

It was a child of Europe who cried this cry,
Oh Holy Ghost what do you mean as to Christ?
I heard him cry. Ah me, the poor child,
Tearing away his heart to be good
Without enchantment. I heard him cry:

Oh Christianity, Christianity,
Why do you not answer our difficulties?
If He was God He was not like us
He could not lose.

Can Perfection be less than perfection?
Can the creator of the Devil be bested by him?
What can the temptation to possess the earth have meant to Him
Who made and possessed it? What do you mean?

And Sin, how could He take our sins upon Him? What does it
 · mean?
To take sin upon one is not the same
As to have sin inside one and feel guilty.

It is horrible to feel guilty,
We feel guilty because we are.
Was He horrible? Did He feel guilty?

You say He was born humble – but He was not,
He was born God –

Taking our nature upon Him. But then you say
He was perfect Man. Do you mean
Perfectly Man, meaning wholly? Or Man without sin? Ah
Perfect Man without sin is not what we are.

Do you mean He did not know that He was God,
Did not know He was the Second Person of the Trinity?
(Oh if He knew this and was,

It was a source of strength for Him we do not have)
But this theology of emptying you preach sometimes –
That He emptied Himself of knowing He was God – seems
A theology of false appearances
To mock your facts, as He was God whether He knew it or not.

Oh what do you mean, what do you mean?
You never answer our difficulties.

You say, Christianity, you say
That the Trinity is unchanging from eternity,
But then you say
At the incarnation He took
Our Manhood into the Godhead
That did not have it before,
So it must have altered it,
Having it.

Oh what do you mean, what do you mean?
You never answer our questions.

So I heard the child of Europe cry,
Tearing his heart away
To be good without enchantment,
Going away bleeding.

Oh how sad it is to give up the Holy Ghost
He is so beautiful, but not when you look close,
And the consolations of religion are so beautiful,
But not when you look close.
Is it beautiful, for instance, is it productive of good
That the Roman Catholic hierarchy should be endlessly discussing
    at this moment
Their shifty theology of birth control, the Vatican
Claiming the inspiration of the Holy Spirit? No, it is not good,

Or productive of good. It is productive
Of contempt and disgust. Yet
On the whole Christianity I suppose is kinder than it was,
Helped to it, I fear, by the power of the Civil Arm.

Oh Christianity, Christianity,
That has grown kinder now, as in the political world
The colonial system grows kinder before it vanishes, are you
    vanishing?
Is it not time for you to vanish?

I do not think we shall be able to bear much longer the dishonesty
Of clinging for comfort to beliefs we do not believe in,
For comfort, and to be comfortably free of the fear
Of diminishing good, as if truth were a convenience.
I think if we do not learn quickly, and learn to teach children,
To be good without enchantment, without the help
Of beautiful painted fairy stories pretending to be true,
Then I think it will be too much for us, the dishonesty,
And, armed as we are now, we shall kill everybody,
It will be too much for us, we shall kill everybody.

THE ASS

In the wood of Wallow
Mash, walked Eugenia, a callow
Girl, they said she was,
An Ass.

Beyond the wood there lay a soppy mórass
But the path across was firm, was
Not a-wash.

Three years in the wood Eugenia stayed
By briar and bramble and lost ways she was delayed,
And in a witch's house within a thicket of yew trees
Was put to work, but seemed so happy that the witch
Finding no pleasure in her tyranny
Gave her release.
She is an ass, she cried, let her pass.
And perish in the soppy mórass.

Eugenia was as happy in the change
To be free to roam and range
As she had been happy and not sad or sorry
At her labours in the witch's bothy.
The sun fell hot upon the causeway
That was not very wide
And the mórass sopped and shuffled
Either side.

And the little beetles ran
About, and all the gnats and the mosquitoes sang
And the mórass was as sweet a green
As Eugenia had ever seen.

She sang: Baa–baa–ba–bay
And seven happy years spent on the way.

Once there came a fiend
Who tempted her to go upon the green
Mórass: Come, ass, and go
Upon the green. But she said, No.
She was not such an ass to try the green,
It would deliver her below.

Heigh-ho, heigh-ho,
Never was such a happy idle ass
Since idleness ran glad in Paradise
As Eugenia was.
Paradise. Paradise.

Now the seven years have passed,
The causeway's ended, the soppy mórass
Has sucked its last; the ass
Comes to a sandy pass
Between low sandhills that are tufted over the esparto grass.
Beyond, the great seas splash
And roll in pleasure to be so a-wash,
Their white crests coming at a dash
To fetch the ass.

Oh my poor ass
To run so quickly as if coming home
To where the great waves crash.
Now she is gone. I thought
Into her tomb.

Yet often as I walk that sandy shore
And think the seas
Have long since combed her out that lies
Beneath, I hear the sweet ass singing still with joy as if
She had won some great prize, as if
All her best wish had come to pass.

A SOLDIER DEAR TO US

It was the War
I was a child
They came from the trenches
To our suburb mild.

Our suburb then was more a country place
They came to our house for release.

In the convalescent Army hospital
That was once a great house and landed estate
Lay Basil, wounded on the Somme,
But his pain was not now so great

That he could not be fetched in a bath-chair
Or hobble on crutches to find in our house there
My mother and aunt, his friends on leave, myself (I was twelve)
And a hearth rug to lie down in front of the fire on and rest
        himself.

It was a November golden and wet
As there had been little wind that year and the leaves were yet
Yellow on the great trees, on the oak trees and elms
Of our beautiful suburb, as it was then.

When Basil woke up he liked to talk and laugh
He was a sweet-tempered laughing man, he said:
'My dear, listen to this' then he read
From The Church Times, how angry the Bishop was because
Of the Reserved Sacrament in the church
Of St Alban's, Holborn. 'Now, my dear' he said, 'for a treat
Next Sunday I will take you to All Saints, Margaret Street; only
You will have to sit on the ladies' side, though you are not yet one
        really.'

Basil never spoke of the trenches, but I
Saw them always, saw the mud, heard the guns, saw the
    duckboards,
Saw the men and the horses slipping in the great mud, saw
The rain falling and never stop, saw the gaunt
Trees and the rusty frame
Of the abandoned gun carriages. Because it was the same
As the poem 'Childe Roland to the Dark Tower Came'
I was reading at school.

Basil and Tommy and Joey Porteous who came to our house
Were too brave even to ask *themselves* if there was any hope
So I laughed as they laughed, as they laughed when Basil said:
What will Ronny do now (it was Ronny Knox) will he pope?

And later, when he had poped, Tommy gave me his book for a
    present,
'The Spiritual Aeneid' and I read of the great torment
Ronny had had to decide, Which way, this or that?
But I thought Basil and Tommy and Joey Porteous were more
    brave than that.

Coming to our house
Were the brave ones. And I could not look at them,
For my strong feelings, except
Slantingly, from the hearth rug, look at them.

Oh Basil, Basil, you had such a merry heart
But you taught me a secret you did not perhaps mean to impart,
That one must speak lightly, and use fair names like the ladies
They used to call
The Eumenides.

Oh Basil
I was a child at school,
My school lessons coloured
   My thoughts of you.

Envoi

Tommy and Joey Porteous were killed in France. Now fifty years
   later
Basil has died of the shots he got in the shell crater
The shrapnel has worked round at last to his merry heart, I write
   this
For a memorial of the soldier dear to us he was.

THE FORLORN SEA

Our Princess married
A fairy King,
It was a sensational
Wedding.

Now they live in a palace
Of porphyry,
Far, far away,
By the fòrlorn sea.

Sometimes people visit them,
Last week they invited me;
That is how I can tell you
They live by a fòrlorn sea.

(They said: Here's a magic carpet,
Come on this,
And when you arrive
We will give you a big kiss.)

I play in the palace garden,
I climb the sycamore tree,
Sometimes I swim
In the fòrlorn sea.

The King and the Princess are shadowy,
Yet beautiful,
They are waited on by white cats,
Who are dutiful.

It is like a dream
When they kiss and cuddle me,
But I like it, I like it,
I do not wish to break free.

So I eat all they give me
Because I have read
If you eat fairy food
You will never wake up in your own bed,

But will go on living,
As has happened to me,
Far, far away
By a fòrlorn sea.

ANGEL BOLEY

There was a wicked woman called Malady Festing
Who lived with her son-in-law, Hark Boley,
And her daughter Angel,
In a house on the high moorlands
Of the West Riding of Yorkshire
In the middle of the last century.

One day Angel
Overheard her mother, Malady, talking to Hark, her husband.
Hark, said Malady, it is time
To take another couple of children
Into our kitchen.
Hark laughed, for he too was wicked and he knew
For what purpose the little children
Were required.

But Angel, who was not happy and so
Lived out her life in a dream of absentmindedness,
In order not to be too much aware
Of her horrible relatives, and what it was
That happened every now and then
In the kitchen; and why the children who came
Were never seen again, this time
When she heard what her husband and mother said,
Came out of her absentmindedness and paid attention.
I know now, she said, and all the time I have known
What I did not want to know, that they kill all children
They lure to this house; and that is why, when I pass in the village,
The people look askance at me, and they whisper –
But not so that I cannot hear –
There goes the daughter of Mother Lure. And the stranger says:
Who is Mother Lure? And they answer: Mrs Festing and they
    make the sign

That is to protect them from evil. Selfish wretches, said Angel,
They do not mind about the children, that evil is not kept from
    them.
Angel wandered into the woods and she said: No more children
Are going to be murdered, and before they are murdered,
    tormented
And corrupted; no more children are going to be the victims
Of Mother Lure and my husband, Hark. Dark was the look then
On Angel's face, and she said: I am the Angel of Death.

Mrs Festing and Boley
Always left the cooking to Angel, they despised Angel but Angel
Could cook, and that they thought was all she was fit for,
To cook and keep house. And they realized
It was far from being to their disadvantage that Angel was,
As they thought, half-witted, and never knew
Or wanted to know, what was going on around her.

As soon as Angel
Said to herself: I am the Angel of Death
She became at once very practical and went out into the woods
    and fields
And gathered some A. Phalloides, commonly called the 'white'
    or deadly
Amanita, a mushroom of high toxicity. These poisonous fungi
She put into a soup, and this soup she gave
To Hark, and her mother, Malady, for supper, so that they died.

Angel then went to the police and said:
I have done evil, but I have saved many children.

The Judge said: Why did you not tell the police
That children were being destroyed? There was no proof, said
    Angel,
Because there were no bodies. I never could find out
What they did with the children after they had killed them.

So then the police searched hard, the wells, the rivers and the
    woodlands,
But never could they find out where
The children lay. Nor had the parents of the children
At any time done anything but weep. For they thought their
    children

Had been bewitched and done away with, and that
If they told their fears of Mother Lure and her wickedness
To the police, they would not believe them, and more children
    than ever
Would disappear.

From then onwards in the trial, Angel spoke
No word more, except to say: I am the Angel of Death.
So they put her in a lunatic asylum, and soon she died
Of an outbreak of typhoid fever. The people of the village
Now loved Angel, because she had delivered them from the fear

Of Mother Lure and Hark Boley, and had saved their
Little children from being tormented and slain by these wicked
    people.
So they wrote on her tombstone: 'She did evil that good
Might come'. But the Vicar said it was better not to put this but
Just her name and age, which was sixteen.
So he had the words
The villagers had written taken off the tombstone. But the next
    day
The words were again on the tombstone; so again the Vicar had
    them
Removed. And this time a watch was set on the grave,
A police constable and the village sexton watched there that
    night.

And no man came again to write on the tombstone
The forbidden words. Yet when morning came,
Again the words were on the tombstone.
So the Vicar said: It is the hand of the Lord.

And now in that graveyard, at that grave's head beneath the yew
    trees,
Still stands today the tombstone of Angel, with the words writ
    on it:
'She did evil that good might come'. May God be merciful.

THE DONKEY

It was such a pretty little donkey
It had such pretty ears
And it used to gallop round the field so briskly
Though well down in years.

It was a retired donkey,
After a life-time of working
Between the shafts of regular employment
It was now free to go merrymaking.

Oh in its eyes was such a gleam
As is usually associated with youth
But it was not a youthful gleam really,
But full of mature truth.

And of the hilarity that goes with age,
As if to tell us sardonically
No hedged track lay before this donkey longer
But the sweet prairies of anarchy.

But the sweet prairies of anarchy
And the thought that keeps my heart up
That at last, in Death's odder anarchy,
Our pattern will be broken all up.
Though precious we are momentarily, donkey,
I aspire to be broken up.

COCK-A-DOO

I love to hear the cock crow in
The middle of the day
It is an eerie sound in
The middle of the day
Sometimes it is a very hot day
Heavy for coming thunder
And the grass I tread on is dusty
And burnt yellow. Away
Over the river Bean which naturally
(It having been hot now for so long)
Runs shallow, stand up
The great yellow cornfields, but
Walking closely by the farm track
Not lifting my head, but foot by
Foot slowly, tired after a long
Walk, I see only the blue
And gray of the flint path, and
Each one of the particles of
Yellow dust on it. And this
Seeing, because of tiredness, becomes
A transfixion of seeing, more sharp
Than mirages are. Now comes the cry
Of the cock at midday
An eerie sound – cook-a-doooo – it

Sharpens a second time
The transfixion. If there were
A third sharpener
Coming this hot day with a butcher's edge
It would spell death.

FRANCESCA IN WINTER

O love sweet love
I feel this love
It burns me so
It comes not from above

It burns me so
The flames run close
Can you not see
How the flames toss

Our souls like paper
On the air?
Our souls are white
As ashes are

O love sweet love
Will our love burn
Love till our love
To ashes turn?

I wish hellfire
Played fire's part
And burnt to end
Flesh soul and heart

Then we could sit beside our fire
With quiet love
Not fear to look in flames and see
A shadow move.

Ah me, only
In heaven's permission
Are creatures quiet
In their condition.

SO TO FATNESS COME

Poor human race that must
Feed on pain, or choose another dish
And hunger worse.

There is also a cup of pain, for
You to drink all up, or,
Setting it aside for sweeter drink,
Thirst evermore.

I am thy friend. I wish
You to sup full of the dish
I give you and the drink,
And so to fatness come more than you think
In health of opened heart, and know peace.

Grief spake these words to me in a dream. I thought
He spoke no more than grace allowed
And no less than truth.

THE SALLOW BIRD

A sallow bird sat on a tree
Yclad in black from head to hee'
And oh he wept sae piteously.

Why sitst thou there and a' so blackit?
Why sitst thou there in thy black jacket,
With feathers furled?

Ah me, ah me,
Come now, tell me.

Then spake the birds in accents sar'
'Something human's dearer far
To me than wealth of a' the world,
And I lack it, and I lack it, I lack it.'

Never seyd he word again
(Nor went away). Yet oft in pain
He'll hauk that crik as if he spak it:
'I lack it, I lack it, I lack it.'

THE WORD

My heart leaps up with streams of joy,
My lips tell of drouth;
Why should my heart be full of joy
And not my mouth?

I fear the Word, to speak or write it down,
I fear all that is brought to birth and born;
This fear has turned my joy into a frown.

He said no word of her to us
Nor we of her to him,
But oh it saddened us to see
How wan he grew and thin.
We said: She eats him day and night
And draws the blood from him,
We did not know but said we thought
This was why he grew thin.

One day we called and rang the bell,
No answer came within,
We said: She must have took him off
To the forest old and grim,
It has fell out, we said, that she
Eats him in forest grim,
And how can we help him being eaten
Up in forests grim?

It is a restless time we spend,
We have no help for him,
We walk about and go to bed,
It is no help to him.
Sometimes we shake our heads and say
It might have better been
If he had spoke to us of her
Or we of her to him.
Which makes us feel helpful, until
The silence comes again.

There was a dog called Clanworthy
Who lived with his friend the cat Hopdance
In the house of Mrs Blow, a widow,
Upon a glade in Cluny.

Hey, Hopdance,
How is Mrs Blow?
So-so, said Hopdance,
Bow, said the dog.

Mrs Blow
Loved her animals very much
She often said:
I do not know what I should do
Without Hopdance and
Clanworthy.

They loved her too.

Hey, Hopdance,
How is Mrs Blow?
So-so, said Hopdance,
She is not very well, said the dog.

Hopdance fetched her a fish
Which she cooked by the fire.
That will do her good,
Said Hopdance; but, said the dog,
She must have wine as well as food.

Clanworthy, brave Clanworthy,
Clanworthy for aye
Through fire and water brought wine
That Mrs Blow might not die.

Mrs Blow has now become their only thought
And care,
All the other animals

In the forest of Cluny
Say there is no talking to them now
Because their only thought is Mrs Blow.
Hey Hopdance,
How is Mrs Blow?
Oh, very well now.
She is quite recovered, said the dog.

But a woodcutter has opined
It was the spirit of Mrs Blow he saw dancing one night
When a full moon fell on the glade of Cluny
With her animals, and that
Clanworthy and Hopdance
Stood upright upon their hind legs
Holding the hand of Mrs Blow the widow
As if she was a child.
If it was Mrs Blow
But he said he thought it was the ghost
Of Mrs Blow, her spirit; and that
The animals, too, did not look like animals; he said
It was three spirits playing ring-a-ring
With crowns on their head.

So everyone remembered then
That a long time ago
The King and Queen had lost their little children
As
A great witch had changed the boys into animals
And the girl into Mrs Blow the widow

Crying: Hopdance, go Hopdance; Clanworthy go,
For a hundred and seven years
Be the animals of Mrs Blow.

Everyone was glad it had come right
And that the princes and the princess
Were dancing in the night.

OH GRATEFUL COLOURS, BRIGHT LOOKS!

The grass is green
The tulip is red
A ginger cat walks over
The pink almond petals on the flower bed.
Enough has been said to show
It is life we are talking about. Oh
Grateful colours, bright looks! Well, to go
On. Fabricated things too – front doors and gates,
Bricks, slates, paving stones – are coloured
And as it has been raining and is sunny now
They shine. Only that puddle
Which, reflecting the height of the sky
Quite gives one a feeling of vertigo, shows
No colour, is a negative. Men!
Seize colours quick, heap them up while you can.
But perhaps it is a false tale that says
The landscape of the dead
Is colourless.

O PUG!

To the Brownes' pug dog, on my lap, in their car,
coming home from Norfolk.

O Pug, some people do not like you,
But I like you,
Some people say you do not breathe, you snore,
I don't mind,
One person says he is always conscious of your behind,
Is that your fault?

Your own people love you,
All the people in the family that owns you
Love you: Good pug, they cry, Happy pug,
Pug-come-for-a-walk.

You are an old dog now
And in all your life
You have never had cause for a moment's anxiety,
Yet,
In those great eyes of yours,
Those liquid and protuberant orbs,
Lies the shadow of immense insecurity. There
Panic walks.

Yes, yes, I know,
When your mistress is with you,
When your master
Takes you upon his lap,
Just then, for a moment,
Almost you are not frightened.

But at heart you are frightened, you always have been.

O Pug, obstinate old nervous breakdown,
In the midst of *so* much love,
And such comfort,
Still to feel unsafe and be afraid,

How one's heart goes out to you!

ARCHIE AND TINA

Archie and Tina
Where are you now,
Playmates of my childhood,
Brother and sister?

When we stayed in the same place
With Archie and Tina
At the seaside,
We used

To paddle the samphire beds, fish
Crabs from the sea-pool, poke
The anemones, run,
Trailing the ribbon seaweed across the sand to the sea's edge
To throw it in as far as we could. We dug
White bones of dead animals from the sandhills, found
The jaw-bone of a fox with some teeth in it, a stoat's skull,
The hind leg of a hare.

Oh, if only; oh, if only!

Archie and Tina
Had a dog called Bam. The silver-sand
Got in his long hair. He had
To be taken home.

Oh, if only . . . !

One day when the wind blew strong
Our dog, Boy, got earache. He had
To be taken home in a jersey.

Oh what pleasure, what pleasure!

There never were so many poppies as there were then,
So much yellow corn, so many fine days,
Such sharp bright air, such seas.

Was it necessary that
Archie and Tina, Bam and Boy,
Should have been there too?
Yes, then it was. But to say now:

Where are you today
Archie and Tina,
Playmates of my childhood,
Brother and sister? Is no more than to say:

I remember
Such pleasure, so much pleasure.

The foolish poet wonders
Why so much honour
Is given to other poets
But to him
No honour is given.

I am much condescended to, said the poet Hin,
By my inferiors. And, said the poet Hin,
On my tombstone I will have inscribed:
'He was much condescended to by his inferiors.'
Then, said the poet Hin,
I shall be properly remembered.

Hin – wiping his tears away, I cried –
Your words tell me
You know the correct use of *shall* and *will*.
That, Hin, is something we may think about,
May, may, may, man.

Well yes, true, said Hin, stopping crying then,
Well yes, but true only in part,
Well, your wiping my tears away
Was a part.

    But ah me, ah me,
So much vanity, said he, is in my heart.
Yet not light always is the pain
That roots in levity. Or without fruit wholly
As from this levity's
Flowering pang of melancholy
May grow what is weighty,
May come beauty.

True too, Hin, true too. Well, as now: You have gone on
Differently from what you begun.
Yet both truths have validity,
The one meanly begot, the other nobly,
And as each alone glosses over
What the other says, so only together
Have they a full thought to uncover.

Over-dew
Became a dread name for Cynthia
In 1937
It was then that Mr Minnim first began to talk openly
About his dear wish.
How dear it was to be
For all of them!

Mr and Mrs Minnim had two sons
Who had done well at school
And won scholarships to Oxford.
Their boyhood was a happy time for all. Then
The elder son married Helen,
A fellow-student at the university,
And, coming down, found a good post with sufficient money.
His wife also
Had money of her own, they were doing well.

The younger son, Georgie,
Was engaged to Cynthia. But that did not go so well.
He took a First in Greats, but then
The difficulties began. He could not find a job.
He did nothing, tried again; no good.
He grew sulky. It seemed hopeless.

It was now that the dread name of Over-Dew
Was spoken,
And a scheme bruited. It was this:
The Minnims were sincere and practising Christians, to
        Mr Minnim
Anyone who was not a Christian
Was a half-educated person.

It was, for instance, suggested
That his daughter-in-law should write a Life of St Benedict,
There was no good life of St Benedict, said Mr Minnim.
So Cynthia suggested that Helen should write it,
Because Helen was a Mediaeval History student,

Whereas Cynthia herself was a Latinist,
So why not Helen, with her special knowledge?
But Helen was not a Christian,
So, 'No', said Mr Minnim, she was a half-educated person.

The Over-Dew scheme was orthodox Christian.
When Mr Minnim retired from his accountancy work
He said that they should move from the suburb where they lived
And buy the house of Over-Dew, which was
A retreat for missionaries to have
On their leave-holidays in England.
And now it was being run, he said, in a fantastical fashion.

When they bought it
Everything would be better,
And different.
Where was the money to come from? No matter,
They had their savings, also they had the faith
Of Mr and Mrs Minnim.

Mrs Minnim loved her husband
And was pleased to follow him to the end of the earth, and
      certainly
Over-Dew was not that.

But oh when Cynthia heard that word
It was the knell
Of all her life and love. This, she said,
Is the end of happy days, and the beginning

Of calamity. Over-Dew, she thought,
Shall be the death of my love and the death of life.
For to that tune, she thought,
Shall come up a European war and personal defeat.

The Georgie situation
Was already sad. What could she do there?

                                       Nothing,
But see him and be silent and so enrage,
Or see him and speak, and the more enrage.
The wise and affectionate Cynthia
Must break the engagement and give back the ring.
There is nothing but this that she can do.
She takes up a post at London University
And in lecturing and study passes the days.
No more of that.

She has read a paper to her pupils
And fellow-dons, the subject is
The development of Latin from the first early growth
Upon the Grecian models. The study entrances,
She finds and reads a Latin prayer:
'I devote to Hades and Destruction'. It is a prayer
For time of battle, the thought is this:
I dedicate the enemy to Hades and Destruction.

                                     And perhaps
One or two of the praying Romans
Will devote also themselves
To Hades and Destruction. Rushing then into battle,
These 'devoted' people hope they may be killed.

                                       If not,
They are held for dead,
They are stateless, and in religion
Have no part at all. The gods have not accepted them,
They are alive, but yet they are destroyed.

In Cynthia's life, this sad year
Was twice as long as all the happy years before.
                                          She must now
Withdraw from Georgie and see him miserable.

She is at work and fast within her family,
The happy careless laughter
Of the brothers and sisters
Rings her round,
She has the home tasks, too,
And thinks of Georgie.

At the end of the year, in the bitter snow that fell that Christmas
The phrenzied Minnims
Moved from their life-long suburb.

The house of Over-Dew
Lay buried half in snow,
It stood five miles from any town upon a hillside.
Very bleak it was, and all the pipes were froze.
Mrs Minnim worked hard,
They had a girl to help them then she left.

Mrs Minnim had courage and was cheerful
But she was by now an old lady. Suddenly
There was the gift of a little money. Mr Minnim
Bought chasubles for visiting priests. But at first
There were no visitors at all, but only
The old cold house, and the lavatories frozen up
And wood kindling to be chopped and dried.
The work was bitter hard.
Mr Minnim, released suddenly
From the routine of his accountancy
Suffered in his head a strange numbness,
He moved about in a dream, would take no hand with the dishes.
    Even

When five-and-twenty missionaries came for a conference
He would do nothing.
He paced the garden plots, 'And here' he said,
'I will build twelve lavatories. And in this room
We will have a consecration and build an altar.'

The thaw came and turned all to mud and slush,
There was still no post for Georgie, he came down from Oxford
And washed the dishes for his mother,
And chopped the wood and moved also in a daze,
The immense learning
Lay off from him, the crude work of the house
Was an excuse from study.

But now Mrs Minnim was not happy, like a sad animal
She roamed the rooms of Over-Dew. This woman
Who had been so boisterous and so loving
With many friends, but still her own best thoughts
For Mr Minnim and their sons,
Was like a sad animal that cannot know a reason

Georgie, with the guilt of the excuse upon his heart,
Grew savage with her. The moody silences
Were shot with cruel words
It was so bitter cold within the house
Though now without the snow was melted and turned to slush.

The money situation preyed upon the mind of Mrs Minnim.

But her husband
Spoke of faith.

In the suburb where they once lived friends said:
How are the Minnims? Did you hear
That Mr Minnim had bought chasubles?

And then the foolish, unkind laughter: Chasubles!
It will be
The ruin of them, the end.

There was one hope that Mrs Minnim had, it was this,
That they might return at last to their house in the suburb,
She had refused to let her husband
Sell this house. No, that she would not allow, No,
That must be for a return.
But now, out of this refusal was made
The bitterness of their life at Over-Dew. For, said her husband,
You kept back the seven hundred and fifty pounds
We might have had for selling the house.

In London
The girl who should have been Georgie's wife
Hears all; understands; loves Georgie; is helpless:
                              reads to her class
The Latin prayer: I devote to Hades and Destruction.
She rules the harsh thoughts that run; cries;
'Come, love of God.'

THE GALLOPING CAT

Oh I am a cat that likes to
Gallop about doing good
So
One day when I was
Galloping about doing good, I saw
A Figure in the path; I said:
Get off! (Be-
cause
I am a cat that likes to
Gallop about doing good)
But he did not move, instead
He raised his hand as if
To land me a cuff
So I made to dodge so as to
Prevent him bring it orf,
Un-for-tune-ately I slid
On a banana skin
Some Ass had left instead
Of putting in the bin. So
His hand caught me on the cheek
I tried
To lay his arm open from wrist to elbow
With my sharp teeth
Because I am
A cat that likes to gallop about doing good.
Would you believe it?
He wasn't there
My teeth met nothing but air,
But a Voice said: Poor cat,
(Meaning me) and a soft stroke
Came on me head
Since when
I have been bald.

I regard myself as
A martyr to doing good.
Also I heard a swoosh
As of wings, and saw
A halo shining at the height of
Mrs Gubbins's backyard fence,
So I thought: What's the good
Of galloping about doing good
When angels stand in the path
And do not do as they should
Such as having an arm to be bitten off
All the same I
Intend to go on being
A cat that likes to
Gallop about doing good
So
Now with my bald head I go,
Chopping the untidy flowers down, to and fro,
An' scooping up the grass to show
Underneath
The cinder path of wrath
Ha ha ha ha, ho,
Angels aren't the only ones who do not know
What's what and that
Galloping about doing good
Is a full-time job
That needs
An experienced eye of earthly
Sharpness, worth I dare say
(If you'll forgive a personal note)
A good deal more
Than all that skyey stuff
Of angels that make so bold as
To pity a cat like me that
Gallops about doing good.

HIPPY-MO

I had a sweet bird
Called Hippy-Mo
But he did not wish to stay
With me, he wished to go.
Hippy-Mo, Hippy-Mo.

I hugged him tight, I said:
You shall not go,
You shall stay here with me
Hippy-Mo.

Then he grew tall as a house,
Hippy-Mo,
Took me in his claws and would
Not let me go,
Hippy-Mo.

His eyes were black as the night
Through which we flew,
And the lightnings flashed from his eyes
As we flew through,
Hippy-Mo what are
You going to do
With me?

Hippy-Mo, Hippy-Mo,
Brought me to a sunny land.
Put me in a cage
Wherein I rage
And when I rage he holds
My hand
So tight I cannot move
From him.

Hippy-Mo
Let me go,
Do you wish me
To die?

He was so mean he did not condescend
To reply. Even
Yes or no.

HENDECASYLLABLES

It is the very bewitching hour of eight
Which is the moment when my new day begins,
I love to hear the pretty clock striking eight
I love to get up out of my bed quickly.
Why is this? Because morning air is so cold?
Or because of new strength that seems to come then?
Both. And also because waking up ends dreams.

BLACK MARCH

I have a friend
At the end
Of the world.
His name is a breath

Of fresh air.
He is dressed in
Grey chiffon. At least
I think it is chiffon.

It has a
Peculiar look, like smoke.

It wraps him round
It blows out of place
It conceals him
I have not seen his face.

But I have seen his eyes, they are
As pretty and bright
As raindrops on black twigs
In March, and heard him say:

I am a breath
Of fresh air for you, a change
By and by.

Black March I call him
Because of his eyes
Being like March raindrops
On black twigs.

(Such a pretty time when the sky
Behind black twigs can be seen
Stretched out in one
Uninterrupted
Cambridge blue as cold as snow.)

But this friend
Whatever new names I give him
Is an old friend. He says:

Whatever names you give me
I am
A breath of fresh air,
A change for you.

GRAVE BY A HOLM-OAK

You lie there, Anna,
In your grave now,
Under a snow-sky,
You lie there now.

Where have the dead gone?
Where do they live now?
Not in the grave, they say,
Then where now?

Tell me, tell me,
Is it where I may go?
Ask not, cries the holm-oak,
Weep, says snow.

How fares it with you, Mrs Cooper my bride?
Long are the years since you lay by my side.
Do you wish I was back? Do you speak of me dearest?
I wish you were back for me to hold nearest.
Who then lies nearer, Mrs Cooper my bride?
A black man comes in with the evening tide.
What is his name? Tell me! How does he dare?
He comes uninvited. His name is Despair.

THE STROKE

For M.

I was a beautiful plant
I stood in the garden supreme
Till there came a blight that fell on each leaf
How I wish this had not been
Oh I wish this had not been.

I can feel the sun, and my blighted leaves
In an elderly way grow glad
But oh in my depths I bleed, I bleed,
From a heart that is youthful and sad
From a heart that is piercèd and sad.

[*The Poem as submitted to the* New Statesman *ended here, but, in an interview with Miss Kay Dick, Stevie Smith added the following two verses orally and they were first published in Kay Dick's* Ivy and Stevie (Duckworth, 1971). *Stevie did not however include them in the version included in* Scorpion *which she had prepared for the press before she was taken ill.*]

Oh, feeling of youth, you had better go,
You are trapped by my age and deceased too.
Goodbye, goodbye, I will send you away,
There is nothing here now to please you.
Then my feeling of youth said, 'No, I will not go;
I will comfort you with love and pain.
And also, if you like, I can procure for you a potion
That you will not take in vain.
The torpors of age could not seize the notion
To drink of the freeing grain, to measure the freeing grain.
All the same, I should not take it if I were you,
As you always can, but rather see life with me through.

It is not very long compared with geological time,
It is heaven to think of geological time.
The weights lifts ... and this gives you a happy mind ...

COME, DEATH (II)

I feel ill. What can the matter be?
I'd ask God to have pity on me,
But I turn to the one I know, and say:
Come, Death, and carry me away.

Ah me, sweet Death, you are the only god
Who comes as a servant when he is called, you know,
Listen then to this sound I make, it is sharp,
Come, Death. Do not be slow.

INDEX OF TITLES

Adelaide Abner 209
A Dream of Comparison 175
A Dream of Nourishment 199
Advice to Young Children 97
A Father for a Fool 72
A House of Mercy 234
A Humane Materialist at the Burning of a Heretic 155
A Jew is Angry with his Friend who does not Believe in Circumcision 153
A King in Funeral Procession 92
Alfred the Great 24
Alone in the Woods 29
A Man I Am 110
A Mother's Hearse 124
I. An Agnostic 201
Analysand 41
'. . . And the Clouds Return After the Rain' 88
Angel Boley 251
Angel of Grace 45
Anger's Freeing Power 181
Après la Politique, La Haine des Bourbons 113
Archie and Tina 264
I. A Religious Man 202
A Shooting Incident 130
At School 211
A Soldier Dear to Us 246
Autumn 95
Avondale 235
Away, Melancholy 187

Bag-Snatching in Dublin 36
Bandol (Var) 23
Behind the Knight 123
Be Off! 104
Bereavement 52
Beware the Man 59

Black March 277
Breughel 60
Brickenden, Hertfordshire 72
But Murderous 194

Can it Be? 214
'Ceci est digne de gens sans Dieu' 116
Childe Rolandine 189
Christmas 120
Cock-a-Doo 255
Come, Death (I) 70
Come Death (II) 282
'Come on, Come Back' 191
Conviction (I) 98
Conviction (II) 99
Conviction (III) 99
Conviction (IV) 99
Cool as a Cucumber 129
Correspondence Between Mr Harrison in Newcastle and Mr Sholto Peach Harrison in Hull 34

Darling Daughters 62
Dear Female Heart 80
Dear Karl 76
Dear Little Sirmio 202
Death Bed of a Financier 149
Death Bereaves Our Common Mother/Nature Grieves for My Dead Brother 36
Death Came to Me 38
Death of Mr Mounsel 53
Death's Ostracism 65
Deeply Morbid 163
Dido's Farewell to Aeneas 189
Die Lorelei 228
Dirge 102
Distractions and the Human Crowd 103

Do Not! 156
Do Take Muriel Out 136
Drugs Made Pauline Vague 145

Egocentric 23
Eng. 35
Es war einmal 31
Eulenspiegelei 63
Evangelie or the Figure of Literary
  Corruption, seeking Glory not
  Truth 223
Every Lovely Limb's a Desolation
  198

Fafnir and the Knights 182
Fallen, Fallen 90
Farewell 229
Forgot! 109
Francesca in Winter 256
Freddy 46
From the Coptic 154
From the County Lunatic Asylum 33
Full Well I Know 162

Girls! 94
Gnädiges Fräulein 85
God and Man 143
God and the Devil 30
God the Drinker 196
Got the Eater 196
Grave by a Holm-Oak 279
'Great Unaffected Vampires and the
  Moon' 203

Happiness 114
Harold's Leap 124
Hast Du Dich Verirrt? 115
Hendecasyllables 277
Hippy-Mo 276
How do you see? 238
How far can you Press a Poet 26
How Slowly Time Lengthens 80
Human Affection 92

I Am 150
'I could let Tom go – but what about
  the children?' 119
If I lie down 98
I Hate this Girl 68

I Like to Play with Him 40
In Canaan's Happy Land 78
Infelice 69
In Protocreation 155
In the Night 111
In the Park 221
I Remember 193
I rode with my darling . . . 142
Is it Wise? 47
It Filled My Heart with Love 20

Jumbo 223

King Hamlet's Ghost 211

Lady 'Rogue' Singleton 105
La Gretchen de Nos Jours (I) 82
Le Majeur Ydow 100
Le Désert de l'Amour 75
Le Revenant 148
Le Singe Qui Swing 138
Lightly Bound 148
Little Boy Lost 44
Little Boy Sick 91
Loin de l'Être 206
Longing for Death because of
  Feebleness 217
Look! 218
Lord Barrenstock 48
Lord Mope 43
Lot's Wife 114
Love Me! 104

Magna est Veritas 220
Major Macroo 50
Man is a Spirit 127
Maximillian Esterhazy 50
Mother, among the Dustbins 7
Mr Over 144
Mrs Blow and Her Animals 266
Mrs Osmosis 55
Mrs Simpkins 25
Murder 93
My Cat Major 207
My Cats 145
My Hat 176
My Heart Goes Out 218
My Soul 79

Nature and Free Animals 35
'N'est-ce pas assez de ne me point
    haïr?' 118
Night-Time in the Cemetery 29
No Categories! 141
No More People 115
No Respect 39
Nor We of Her to Him 259
Not Waving but Drowning 167
Nourish Me on an Egg 83
Numbers 32

Oh grateful colours, bright looks!
    262
O Happy Dogs of England 61
Oh, If Only . . . 160
'Oh stubborn race of Cadmus'
    seed. . .' 134
One of Many 65
On the Death of a German
    Philosopher 22
O Pug! 263
Our Bog is Dood 146
Out of Time 88

Papa Love Baby 22
Parents 208
Parrot 67
Persephone 134
Poet! 95
Private Means is Dead 51
Proud Death with Swelling Port 78

Quand on n'a pas ce que l'on aime,
    il faut aimer ce que l'on a – 101

Rencontres Funestes 105
Reversionary 76
Road Up 54

Saint Anthony and the Rose of Life
    180
Satin-Clad 116
Scorpion 236
Seymour and Chantelle or Un peu
    de vice 237
She said 101
Silence and Tears 71
Song d'Athalie 184

So to fatness come 257
Souvenir de Monsieur Poop 83
Spanish School 27
Study to Deserve Death 102
Suburb 57
Sunt Leones 42

Tender Only to One 61
The Abominable Lake 64
The Actress 108
The After-Thought 139
The Airy Christ 200
The Ambassador 134
The Ass 243
The Bereaved Swan 33
The Bishops of the Church of England
    62
The Blue from Heaven 171
The Boat 67
The Bottle of Aspirins 106
The Broken Friendship 139
The Castle 122
The Celtic Fringe 158
The Celts 204
The Children of the Cross 90
The Choosers 224
The Commuted Sentence 157
The Conventionalist 101
The Crown of Bays 151
The Death Sentence 157
The Deserter 142
The Devil-my-Wife 108
The Doctor 68
The Donkey 254
The Engine Drain 177
The English 210
The English Visitor 168
The Face 97
The Failed Spirit 118
The Fairy Bell 169
The Film Star 106
The Fool 115
The Forlorn Sea 248
The Friend 86
The Frog Prince 232
The Fugitive's Ride 55
The Galloping Cat 274

285

The Ghost of Ware 166
The Governess 107
The Hat 149
The Hostage 185
The Hound of Ulster 21
The House of Over-Dew 268
The Jungle Husband 190
The Lads of the Village 87
The Lady from the Well-Spring
  173
The Leader 159
The Light of Life 221
The Little Daughters of America
  101
The Magic Morning 111
The Murderer 74
The New Age 170
The Occasional Yarrow 225
The Old Sweet Dove of Wiveton
  215
The Orphan Reformed 130
The Passing Cloud 205
The Past 216
The Photograph 87
The Pleasures of Friendship 113
The Poet Hin 266
The Poets Are Silent 113
The Queen and the Young Princess
  175
The Reason 40
The Recluse 119
The Rehearsal 149
The Repentance of Lady T 108
The Ride 150
The River Deben 37
The River God 128
The River Humber 81
The Roman Road 121
The Sallow Bird 258
The Sea-Widow 280
The Singing Cat 216
The Sliding Mountain 118
The Smile 109
The Sorrowful Girl 225
The Starling 227
The Stroke 281
The Suburban Classes 27

The Violent Hand 92
The Virtuoso 100
The Wanderer 140
The Weak Monk 137
The White Thought 111
The Wild Dog 104
The Word 258
The Zoo 95
This Englishwoman 48
This is Disgraceful and Abominable
  194
Thought is Superior 128
Thoughts about the Person from
  Porlock 230
To a Dead Vole 76
To a Lady in a Train 209
To an American Publisher 149
To Dean Inge Lecturing on Origen
  123
Torquemada 121
To School! 148
To the Tune of the Coventry Carol
  26
Touch and Go 125

Unpopular, lonely and loving 116
Unser Vater 85

Villains 100
Voices about the Princess Anemone
  163
Voices against England in the Night
  117

'What is she writing? Perhaps it will
  be good' 169
When the Sparrow Flies 116
Where are you going? 94
Who is this Who Howls and Mutters?
  219
Who Killed Lawless Lean? 53
Who Shot Eugenie? 160
Why are the Clergy ...? 193
Will Ever? 90
Will Man Ever Face Fact and not
  Feel Flat? 197
Wretched Woman 147

INDEX OF FIRST LINES

A child is born, they cry, a child   120
A couple of women is one too many   115
Across the bridge across the dyke   55
A dark rose grew in the desert   180
Adelaide Abner is cruel   209
A dismal bell hung in the belfry   169
Admirals Curse-You and No-More   101
All the waters of the river Deben   37
Alone in the woods I felt   29
A mother slew her unborn babe   194
An antique story comes to me   228
Angel most cynical   92
Archie and Tina   264
A sallow bird sat on a tree   258
A thousand and fifty-one waves   32
At school I always walk with Elwyn   211
Away, melancholy   187

Bandol (Var)   23
Behind the Knight sits hooded Care   123
Beware the man whose mouth is small   59

Can it be, can it be   214
'Children who paddle where the ocean bed shelves steeply'
   97
Christ died for God and me   98
Cold as no love, and wild with all negation   101
Cold as No Plea   157
Coleridge received the Person from Porlock   230
Come, wed me, Lady Singleton   105
Cool as a cucumber calm as a mill pond sound as a bell   129
Count Flanders   113

Dark was the day for Childe Rolandine the artist   189
Darling daughters, listen to your mother   62
Deal not with me God as I have dealt with Man   149
Dearest Evelyn, I often think of you   190
Dear female heart, I am sorry for you   80
Dear Karl, I send you Walt Whitman in a sixpenny book
   76

Dear little Sirmio   202

Death came to me and said   38

Deep in the mysterious waters of the lake a world lies
    drowned   64

Deeply morbid deeply morbid was the girl who typed the
    letters   163

Donnez à manger aux affamées   106

Do not despair of man, and do not scold him   156

Do take Muriel out   136

Drugs made Pauline vague   145

'Eh bien! Marche!', fit le Majeur Ydow   100

England, you had better go   117

Fair waved the golden corn   78

Farewell dear friends   229

Farewell for ever, well for ever fare   93

Far from normal far from normal far from normal I am
    150

Fourteen-year-old, why must you giggle and dote   101

From a friend's friend I taste friendship   102

Full well I know the flinty heart   162

Girls! although I am a woman   94

God and the Devil   30

Happiness is silent, or speaks equivocally for friends   114

Harold, are you asleep?   124

He blinks he sighs   92

He chases his tail   41

He is quite captive to the Lady of the Well-Spring   173

He often gazes on the air   201

He said no word of her to us   259

He says that religious thought and all our nerviness   202

He told his life story to Mrs Courtly   95

He trod in dream upon the brim   65

He wrote *The I and the It*   22

Honour and magnify this man of men   24

How do you see the Holy Spirit of God?   238

How far can you press a poet   26

How fares it with you, Mrs Cooper my bride   280

How nice it is to slink the streets at night   57

How slowly time lengthens from a hated event   80

How sweet the birds of Avondale   235

I admire the Bishops of the Church of England   62

I always admire a beautiful woman   149

288

I am a frog   232
I am becalmed in a deep sea   218
I am dying Egypt dying   53
I am not God's little lamb   91
I am sorry to say my dear wife is a dreamer   104
I am that Persephone   134
I am the self-appointed guardian of English literature   83
I can't say I enjoyed it, but the pay was good   108
I cry I cry   141
I fear the ladies and gentlemen under the trees   105
I feel a mortal isolation   198
I feel ill. What can the matter be   282
If I lie down upon my bed I must be here   98
I had a dream of nourishment   199
I had a dream three walls stood up wherein a raven bird
     181
I had a sweet bird   276
I hate this girl   68
I have a friend   277
I have lived and followed my fate without flinching,
     followed it gladly   189
I have no respect for you   39
I like to get off with people   99
I like to play with him   40
I like to see him drink the gash   196
I like to toss him up and down   145
I longed for companionship rather   111
I long for the desolate valleys   114
'I look at the bottle when mournful I feel'   106
I look in the glass   108
I look in the mirror   166
I love my beautiful hat more than anything   149
I love to hear the cock crow in   255
I married the Earl of Egremont   122
I may be smelly and I may be old   128
In a shower of tears I sped my fears   88
In his fur the animal rode, and in his fur he strove   201
In protocreation   155
In the cold light of morning she was looking rather queer
     85
In the flame of the flickering fire   79
In the graveyard, in the graveyard   168
In the quiet waters   182
In the wood of Wallow   243
I raised my gun   31
I rode with my darling in the dark wood at night   142
I shall be glad to be silent, Mother, and hear you speak   111

Is it wise   47

I think of the Celts as rather a whining lady   204

I thought as I lay on my bed one night, I am only a passing
   cloud   205

It is a formal and deserted garden   88

It is the bird of burial   134

It is the very bewitching hour of eight   277

It seemed a curious place to rest one's body and take one's
   ease   54

It was a dream and shouldn't I bother about a dream   184

It was a graveyard scene. The crescent moon   203

It was a house of female habitation   234

It was a little captive cat   216

It was a mile of greenest grass   225

It was my bridal night I remember   193

It was such a pretty little donkey   254

It was the mighty Engine Drain, the Engine Drain, the
   Engine Drain   177

It was the War   246

I walked abroad in Easter Park   99

I want to be your pinkie   75

I was a beautiful plant   281

I was consumed by so much hate   110

I was talking one day   45

I will forgive you everything   35

I will never leave you darling   227

Jumbo, Jumbo, Jumbo darling, Jumbo come to Mother
   223

Kathleen ni Houlihan   158

King Arthur rode in another world   171

Lamb dead, dead lamb   36

Left by the ebbing tide of battle   191

Let all the little poets be gathered together in classes   148

Listen, all of you, listen, all of you   123

Little boy   21

Little Master Home-from-School   72

Lord Barrenstock and Epicene   48

Love me, Love me, I cried to the rocks and the trees   104

Major Hawkaby Cole Macroo   50

Major is a fine cat   207

Man does not live by bread alone   130

Man is a spirit. This the poor flesh knows   127

Man is coming out of the mountains   125

Man is my darling, my love and my pain   143
Many of the English   210
Maria Holt   52
Men fear the hollow men at the top of the tree   159
Mother, among the dustbins and the manure   74
Mother, I love you so   92
Mother, mother, let me go   175
Mother said if I wore this hat   176
Mr Over is dead   144
Mrs Osmosis   55
Mrs Simpkins never had very much to do   25
My child, my child, watch how he goes   115
My heart goes out to my Creator in love   218
'My heart is fallen in despair'   139
My heart leaps up with streams of joy   258
My life is vile   40
My mother was a romantic girl   22
My soul within the shades of night   119
My true love breathed her latest breath   74
My Uncle from the realms of Death   148

Never again will I weep   44
Nobody heard him, the dead man   167
Nobody knows what I feel about Freddy   46
Nourish me on an egg, Nanny   83
No wonder   81
Now Vole art dead   76

Of all the disgraceful and abominable things   194
O happy dogs of England   61
Oh cold and ferocious are the children of the cross   90
Oh ho uncircumciséd Sadducee I see   153
Oh I am a cat that likes to   274
Oh Lion in a peculiar guise   121
Oh where are you going ye human faces   94
Oh would that I were a reliable spirit careering about   217
O love sweet love   256
O Maximilian stern and wild   50
O Pug, some people do not like you   263
Ormerod was deeply troubled   103
Our Bog is dood, our Bog is dood   146
Our Princess married   249
Outside the house   138
Over-dew   268

Parents who barely can afford it   208
Passing at my pleasure's pace   115

People who are always praising the past   216
Poet, thou art dead and damned   95
Poor human race that must   257
Poor noble Ghost that comes from place of pain   211
Private means is dead   51
Profit and Batten   100
Proud Death with swelling port comes ruffling by   78
Pull my arm back, Seymour   237
Put out that Light   221

Rapunzel Rapunzel let down your hair   139
Riding slowly along the banks of a canal   150

Satin-clad, with many a pearl   116
Shall I tell you the signs of a New Age coming   170
She said as she tumbled the baby in   101
She's not Indian, she's ill   209
Sholto Peach Harrison you are no son of mine   34
Shut me not alive away   157
Since what you want, not what you ought   119
Sisley   36
Sitting alone on a summer's evening   72
Stand off, Mother, let me go!   118
Study to deserve Death, they only may   102

Tender only to one   61
The ages blaspheme   60
The angel that rebellion raised   90
The boating party   111
The boat took my love away   67
The City Dog goes to the drinking trough   104
The foolish poet wonders   266
The funeral paths are hung with snow   29
The grass is green   262
The intellectual Englishman shrank away from the bedside   160
The lads of the village, we read in the lay   87
The lion dishonoured bids death come   76
The lion sits within his cage   95
The lions who ate the Christians on the sands of the arena   42
The love of a mother for her child   124
The milky love of this bland child   107
The monk sat in his den   137
The nearly right   26
The nervous face of my dear wife   108
The old sick green parrot   67

The orphan is looking for parents   130
The painters of Spain   27
The parrot   53
The people say that spiritism is a joke and a swizz   33
The pleasures of friendship are exquisite   113
The portrait of my mother   100
There is a face I know too well   97
There is a fearful solitude   109
There is a god in whom I do not believe   196
There is far too much of the suburban classes   27
There's no new spirit abroad   113
There was a dog called Clanworthy   260
There was a wicked woman called Malady Festing   251
The rocks and trees in silence stood   197
These hands so well articulated   116
The shadow was so black   99
The tears of the widow of the military man   71
The terrors of the scenery   118
The wood was rather old and dark   44
The world is come upon me, I used to keep it a long way
    off   142
They gave him a crown of bays and dressed him up   151
They photographed me young upon a tiger skin   87
This Englishwoman was so refined   48
'This night shall thy soul be required of thee'   236
Thought is superior to dress and circumstance   128
Three angels came to the red red clay   154
To be so cold and not yet old   63
To those who are isolate   118
'Twas the voice of the sweet dove   215
'Twas the voice of the wanderer, I heard her exclaim   140
Two ladies walked on the soft green grass   175

Uncle Torquemada   121
Underneath the broad hat is the face of the Ambassador
    134
Underneath the tangled tree   163
Unpopular, lonely and loving   116
Unser Vater   85

Walking one day in the park in winter   221
Walking swiftly with a dreadful duchess   69
Wan   33
We had ridden three days Eugenie and I   160
We needs must love the highest when we see it   86
What care I if good God be   23
What has happened to the young men of Eng.   35

What is she writing?   Perhaps it will be good   169
What shall we say of this curious young man   43
When ancient girl is garbed in spite   109
When shall that fuel fed fire grow fatter   155
When the sparrow flies to the delicate branch   116
Who is this that comes in splendour, coming from the
    blazing East   200
Who is this that howls and mutters   219
Who shall we send to fetch him away   224
Why are the clergy of the Church of England   193
Why dost thou dally, Death, and tarry on the way   70
Wicked and corrupt   223
Will ever the stormy seas and the surges deep   90
With my looks I am bound to look simple or fast I would
    rather look simple   220
Would he might come   82
Wretched woman that thou art   147

You are not looking at all well, my dear   68
You are only one of many   65
You beastly child, I wish you had miscarried   148
You don't look at all well, quite loin de l'être in fact   206
You hang at dawn, they said   185
You lie there, Anna   279
You say I must write *another* book? But I've just written
    this one   149

MORE ABOUT PENGUINS
AND PELICANS

Penguinews, which appears every month, contains details of all the new books issued by Penguins as they are published. From time to time it is supplemented by our stocklist which includes around 5,000 titles.

A specimen copy of *Penguinews* will be sent to you free on request. Please write to Dept EP, Penguin Books Ltd, Harmondsworth, Middlesex, for your copy.

In the U.S.A.: For a complete list of books available from Penguins in the United States write to Dept CS, Penguin Books, 625 Madison Avenue, New York, New York 10022.

In Canada: For a complete list of books available from Penguins in Canada write to Penguin Books Canada Ltd, 2801 John Street, Markham, Ontario L3R 1B4.